Without Offending Humans

posthumanities

Cary Wolfe SERIES EDITOR

(continued on page 158)

Without Offending Humans

A Critique of Animal Rights

Élisabeth de Fontenay

Translated by Will Bishop

posthumanities 24

UNIVERSITY OF MINNESOTA PRESS

MINNEAPOLIS

LONDON

This work, published as part of a program providing publication assistance, received financial support from the French Ministry of Foreign Affairs, the Cultural Services of the French Embassy in the United States, and FACE (French American Cultural Exchange). www.frenchbooknews.com

French Voices Logo designed by Serge Bloch

Portions of Martin Heidegger, *Introduction to Metaphysics,* trans. Gregory Fried and Richard Polt (New Haven, Conn.: Yale University Press, 2000) copyright 2000 by Yale University. Reprinted by permission of Yale University Press.

Excerpt from "Ballade" from *The Poems of François Villon,* trans. Galway Kinnell copyright 1965, 1977 by Galway Kinnell. Reprinted by permission of Houghton Mifflin Harcourt Publishing Company. All rights reserved.

Originally published in French as *Sans offenser le genre humain: Réflexions sur la cause animale.* Copyright 2008 by Éditions Albin Michel.

English translation copyright 2012 by the Regents of the University of Minnesota

Published by the University of Minnesota Press
111 Third Avenue South, Suite 290
Minneapolis, MN 55401–2520
http://www.upress.umn.edu

Library of Congress Cataloging-in-Publication Data
Fontenay, Élisabeth de.
[Sans offenser le genre humain. English]
Without offending humans : a critique of animal rights /
Élisabeth de Fontenay ; translated by Will Bishop.
(Posthumanities ; 24)
Includes bibliographical references and index.
ISBN 978-0-8166-7604-0 (hc : alk. paper)
ISBN 978-0-8166-7605-7 (pb : alk. paper)
1. Human–animal relationships—Philosophy. 2. Animals and civilization—Philosophy. 3. Animals (Philosophy). I. Title.
QL85.F6613 2012
599.15—dc23
2012018076

Printed in the United States of America on acid-free paper

The University of Minnesota is an equal-opportunity educator and employer.

19 18 17 16 15 14 13 12   10 9 8 7 6 5 4 3 2 1

for

Animals do not know we have given them names.

—ELIAS CANETTI

Contents

Preface

Brother humans who live after us
Don't let your hearts harden against us
For if you have pity on wretches like us
More likely God will show mercy to you

—FRANÇOIS VILLON, "Ballade"

With only a slight modification to the first verse of this stanza, a change to only one word, an animal's plea can be heard in these lines: *Brother humans who live with us* . . . The stanza takes on a different meaning that does not, however, exclude its initial one. For the term "humanity" is actually tormented by two senses: the sense of *humankind,* but also the sense of an unlimited *goodness.* I have lodged the following pages at the heart of this semantic ambiguity.

Six of the seven chapters the reader finds gathered here were written after the publication of the *Silence of the Beasts,*[1] and chapter 1, which touches on Derrida's posthumous work, appears here for the first time. I have freely modified or completed these texts, which were originally conference papers, lectures, or contributions to collective works or journals. If all of the chapters are haunted by "the trauma of birth,"[2] which ties all men[3] *in particular* to certain beasts, they are of course pronounced with very different emphases. One does not speak with the same accent about cruelty toward beasts in front of a large audience and about three episodes of lesser boorishness toward animals over the course of the history of reason for a philosophical society. Or, to take yet another example, it is one thing to let oneself get angry over the so-called "bio" arts and quite a different thing to analyze the racist abominations of animalization.

In *Silence of the Beasts* I paid sustained attention to the decisive experience of identity and alterity brought about by the fate of an equivocal philosophical notion, the *animal,* and its effects on the tradition of Western philosophy as a whole. Within this trajectory, I was experimenting with a reading of the history of philosophy, one that sought to be different: a deconstruction placed under the sign of a Borgesian animal, the Goofus Bird, "which builds its nest upside-down and flies backwards, because it doesn't give a darn where it's going, it only wants to know where it's been."[4] The animal question was at the time one that involved "physical science, morals and poetics."[5] In the following pages, it transforms into a question of physical science, morals, and politics.

The center of gravity shifted because it had become inevitable, after the fact, to address the question referred to as "zoo-anthropological" difference, the one I had intentionally not treated. It was therefore necessary to account for this subject without backtracking, by which I mean without denying my engagement on behalf of animals. But how then could I not allow myself to be caught up in the proper of man, that metaphysical catechism that is useless to humans and destructive to beasts, one that I, in turn, had relentlessly deconstructed? And, alternately, how was I to keep materialism from sliding into continuist, naturalist, positivist, reductionist, physicalist, eliminationist distortions? I have often told myself that if these attempts, and especially the program for a naturalization of spirit, encountered such a deep-seated rejection in me, it's because a certain way of thinking about the human exception was not all so foreign to me and that I would one day have to provide further explanation.

This is why the following chapters find their rhythm thanks to the oscillations of a concern, the *Unruhe* Leibniz compares to the beat of the clock. Nowhere do I cease persevering with a claim in favor of animals, by recalling their kinship with us and our inequity toward them, but as I do so, I try to allow a continuous descant to be heard, one that has always undergirded my work and whose monotonous phrasing sketches out a humanism that is both uncompromising and emptied of all determination.

This is why, if it sometimes happens that, backed into a corner, I suggest that we recognize certain singularities of human reality, it is first of all to calm things down by awakening, in beings I will never consent to define as human animals, the mysterious responsibility of good will toward beasts. That good will that Rimbaud describes when he enigmatically writes: "Thief of fire. Humanity is his responsibility, even the animals."[6]

1

Their Secret Elect

I am saying "they," "what they call an animal," in order to mark clearly the fact that I have always secretly exempted myself from that world, and to indicate that my whole history, the whole genealogy of my questions, in truth everything that I am, follow, think, write, trace, erase even, seems to me to be born from that exceptionalism and incited by that sentiment of election. As if I were the secret elect of what they call animals.

—JACQUES DERRIDA, *The Animal That Therefore I Am*

"The philosopher, the one the animal does not look at" . . . When, for the first time, I heard Jacques Derrida speak at the Collège de philosophie, directed at the time by Jean Wahl, I reacted, all things being relative, as Malebranche did upon reading Descartes's *Treatise on Man:* "His beating heart sometimes forced him to stop his reading," writes Fontenelle. From that moment on, I did not take leave of this work nor of this man, even if it would often cause me distress to place myself in certain of his footsteps.

But in a way, I missed out on the first traces of Derridean thinking about animals, for it is only after hearing and then reading *On Spirit* in 1987 that I was able to measure the force and permanence of this insistence, and then, yet again, in 2001, in the dialogue with Elisabeth Roudinesco.[1]

As for me, I had spent twenty years thinking about *beasts,* stirred by a desire to confront certain familiar experiences with what, throughout the ages, philosophers had written about animals. "La raison du plus fort," a long preface to a French edition of Plutarch's *Three Treatises for Animals,* had appeared in 1992, then *The Silence of the Beasts* in 1999.

1

I didn't participate in the Cerisy conference devoted to Derrida, whose acts were published under the title *L'animal autobiographique* at the end of 1999. It was only with their publication that I discovered the introduction he had delivered before his paper. After his death and under the title *L'animal que donc je suis* (*The Animal That Therefore I Am*), the totality of his intervention was published.

All of this is to say, in the most modest way possible, that on this question, my thinking was both parallel and asymptotic to his, and that I would not be able to publish the texts I wrote and pronounced in the wake of *The Silence of the Beasts* without first meditating on what, from him, appeared subsequent to the publication of my own book. For these are words I did not *know* how to hear, and then a text that I was *unable* to read in time. It's a matter of debt and of dates.

"Of the animal who comes to Derrida": this would be one blasphemous yet friendly way of parodying the title of a major text by Levinas: *Of God Who Comes to Mind*. The animal, from the moment it infiltrated Derrida to accomplish its work, functioned not as a topos or a philosopheme, but as a major trope, a resource for arguments in the service of the deconstruction of what is proper to man: humanist metaphysics and its authoritarian rhetoric, the rhetoric that persists for example, and par excellence, in Heidegger, when he establishes a variously described abyss between the "merely living" and the *Dasein*. Trace, writing, grapheme: these are the operators of what, from the very beginning of the grammatological enterprise, allowed for the opposition human/nonhuman to be exceeded/preceded. The new concept of the trace was destined to spread to the entire field of the living, beyond the anthropological limits of language, the limits of phonologocentrism. This is why, in his later texts, Derrida constantly recalls, in a kind of auto-bio-bibliography, just how and how much the animal and animals had always already slipped into his work. Without in any way suggesting a periodization of the work—something that would come off as a serious misinterpretation—I will be distinguishing among three levels of deconstruction that are, even as they interpenetrate one another, testimony to the radicalization and shift of argument: a strategy *through* the animal, exposition *to* an animal or *to this* animal, and compassion *toward* animals.

Strategy, to start with. The animal first of all insinuates itself like a Trojan horse into the metaphysics that runs from Descartes to Levinas. It allows for an operation of rupture aiming at erasing or, even better, at overturning the so-called anthropological boundary. Of all the oppositions placed back to back that Derrida sets into place, the one between man and animal is the most decisive: one could say that it is the opposition that commands the others. For Derrida, it is a question of showing how an invariant repeatedly occurs as a way of folding the Heideggerian conception of *Dasein* into the Cartesian and Hegelian metaphysical humanisms: language, hands, spirit, and death, but also becoming-subject, historicity, leaving the state of nature, sociality, and access to knowledge and to technique. These are the ways the metaphysical tradition has indefinitely re-marked a subjugating superiority of man over animal that can take the form both of a "projection that appropriates" and an "interruption that excludes."[2]

In the most recent version of this deconstruction of the man/ animal division, one notes the determinate manner with which a generality, *the animal,* or, what comes down to more or less the same thing, of a tropological bestiary—animal figures—transforms into a multiplicity, *animals,* an immensely effective and effectuated multiplicity of *other* living beings that does not allow itself to be homogenized into the category of animal without violence or motivated ignorance. Derrida in no way denies that there is something like an *abyss* between men and animals—he even uses the Heideggerian word. But against doxic and metaphysical evidence concerning the clarity and linearity of this separation, he proposes what he calls a limitrophy (from *trephein,* "to feed" in Greek). Thanks to a subversive topic, this concept allows him to think about what lies near limits, what limitations nourish and allow to grow at their edges, and what complicates them indefinitely. Limits are layered, plural, folded over one another, and heterogeneous, and they do not allow for a determination of anything as completely objectifiable.

Hence, it is with the same gesture that he dismisses continuism and discontinuism; continuism—associated with a certain analytical, naturalistic, objectivist philosophy—is dismissed with particular disdain when it is treated as sleepwalking and asinine.[3]

What I have just described is the deconstruction of a certain epochal configuration: that of phallagocentrism, in other words the deconstruction of an unvarying schema of anthropocentric teleology that functions from Descartes to Levinas by way of Kant, Hegel, Heidegger, and Lacan. Yet there is a second level of deconstruction, unrelated to the history of metaphysics: the *quasi timeless* configuration of carnophallogocentrism, of a matrix of the symbolic, since before time, "since time, since so long ago, hence since all of time and for what remains of it to come."[4] Over the course of an interview with Jean-Luc Nancy titled "'Eating Well,' or the Calculation of the Subject,"[5] an interview that bears on carnivorousness, Derrida underlines the fact that the Decalogue mentions *only* the prohibition of homicide. And, in this denial of the murder of the animal, he sees the necessary and violent condition for the institution both of the subject and of the other. There would thus be a Judaic as well as a Greek sacrificial structure, a quasi-transcendental of the advent of the *self-designated* human. Derrida here maximizes the use of the animal trope; he hyperbolizes it, in ways comparable to the use Descartes made of the "evil genius."

It would be an exaggeration to say that there is between this first layer and the second—the one I am calling *exposition to an animal, to that animal*—the mark of a qualitative leap, or even of a turn. One can only ask if the animal remains merely a tool of deconstruction. For as this work is written and spoken, it is going to be more and more often a question of *this or that* animal on the one hand and, on the other, animals *in general.* What happens then is that the singular—this animal here—or the plural—animals—breaks into the discourse, something that is not foreign to the proliferation of borders that escapes ontology's control. This branch can be seen at work in two texts in which Derrida *has recourse* to the animal as if the animal were coming to him.

A first occurrence is found in the interview called "What Is Poetry?": "Not the phoenix, not the eagle,"[6] he answers, but the hedgehog. This humble mammal is appealed to as a catachresis of the poem, as if there were no word other than this metaphor to designate this thing, the poem, the proper of which would be the way the poem is "not reappropriable into the family of the subject."[7] The hedgehog, "a suckling hedgehog, perhaps,"[8] is here, therefore, to represent the grounding humility of the poem and to be on the lookout for an answer, careful to escape ontological Heideggerian recuperations of the poetic. Then off it goes, this hedgehog, as if it had escaped its rhetorical enclosure. Something like a real animal seizes the figurative one when it so happens that this little mammal gets run over in the middle of the highway, "rolled up in a ball, turned toward the other and toward itself . . . its arrows held at the ready, when this ageless blind thing hears but does not see death coming. . . . Humble and close to the ground, it can only expose itself . . . It has no relation to itself—that is no totalizing individuality—that does not expose it even more to death and to being-torn-apart."[9]

Derrida relates a reference Heidegger made to a Grimm brothers' fairytale, "The Hedgehog and the Hare." In order to be sure of winning his race against the hare, the hedgehog sends its female to the finish line so that she can cry out "I am here!" Heidegger staged this "I am here" in *Identity and Difference* as a way of illustrating the "always already there" of the *Dasein*.[10] Derrida writes that, to the contrary, his hedgehog "can barely say '*Ich*' and certainly not '*bünn*,' still less '*hier*' and '*da*.'"[11] This does not mean, he adds, that it is deprived of speech, but that "there is, in the end, no cogito or work for this hedgehog who cannot gather itself together enough to say '*Ich bin hier*' or '*ergo sum*.'"[12] What then begins to insist, in an irrepressible way, is the proposition according to which "being-for-death," like "being-thrown," is the fate not just of men but of all living things: this proposition is a significant rupture, for it inaugurates a community of mortal living beings. And it does so against Heidegger, for whom "being-for-death" is in no way the being of something simply living, which can only end: only *Dasein*, along

with speech, detains the monopoly on relating to death as such—
and therefore of *dying*.

It is as if this text throws the metaphorical hedgehog into the
precipice of proper meaning, onto the highway, under the cars that
run over it. It is in effect as if the catachrestic representation of the
poem had, according to Derrida, turned tautegorical. The revelation
of an *Ereignis also henceforth* bears on that animal and no longer concerns only the poem.[13] Heidegger would say that the hedgehog does
not see death coming, that death does not happen to it. Derrida
says this, too, but in an entirely different way. The hedgehog "'hears
but does not see death coming,' it is as blind as Homer."[14] Where,
he wonders, is the limit drawn? "Is it certain that the human *Dasein*
sees death coming *as such? *What is the 'as such' in the case of death?
And how can one maintain that the hedgehog has no apprehension
of death when it rolls itself up in a ball?"[15] This is the first time, or
at least I think it is, that a singular animal, in the body and in the
flesh, is presented this way in his writing, and it's moving.

A second time, an animal just as singular, a unique one even,
barges in, and the operation of deconstruction, turning autobio-
graphical, changes style and tone. For it is no longer merely the representation of an anonymous individual belonging to a singular
species that comes to Derrida—in other words, a hedgehog destined to die run over—but "the gaze of a seer, a visionary or extra-
lucid blind,"[16] the gaze of a truly real cat, his cat, an irreplaceable
living being, an existence resistant to any concept. He sees himself
suddenly being looked at *naked* by this animal in the bathroom.
At this point a brief drama of immense dispossession is played
out, a drama of *depropriation,* over the course of which Heidegger
and Levinas find themselves dismissed back to back, for this scene
overturns both the Heideggerian non-gaze of the animal and the
Levinasian prescription-event of the other's face. The fact of *seeing
oneself seen naked* by the depthless gaze of this absolute alterity is
an experience that, as Derrida repeatedly declares, is before time,
before any questioning about the other as a neighbor, equal, or
enemy. Such a poetic and prophetic situation ends up provoking a
vertiginous series of questions.

This little story, this entirely novel experience of modesty and nudity when confronted with an animal gaze,[17] will give rise in the Derridean text to an incredible reading of the major story of the appellation scene that is played out in Genesis, when, as if for the first time, one finds the exposition of the triangularity God—man—beasts. Derrida places the two creation stories in Genesis in opposition to one another. In the first, man is created as both man and woman, and his mission is to *subjugate* animals. In the second, man is *Isch,* without *Ischa,* and God orders him only to *name* the animals. It is through a meditation in turn on what serves as a foundation, by attaching himself to the letter of this second story—and I cite once more his words, "since time, since so long ago, hence since all of time and for what remains of it to come"[18]—that he is going to suggest how seeing, naming, calling, and responding to the call are articulated in relation to one another.

This is a text that must be read, as Derrida invites us to do, alongside Walter Benjamin's "On Language as Such and on the Language of Man."[19] For, he writes, "the public crying of names remains *at one and the same time* free *and* overseen," and God "lets Adam . . . freely call out the names. . . . But he is waiting around the corner, watching over this man alone with a mixture of curiosity and authority."[20] In the version of Genesis that says that God had the animals come *to see* how man will call them, it is as if, Derrida comments, he wanted both to "oversee, keep vigil, maintain his right of inspection over the names that would shortly begin to resound . . . but also to abandon himself to his curiosity, even allow himself to be surprised and outflanked by the radical novelty of what was going to occur, by this irreversible . . . event of naming"[21]—by the birth of a poet, in sum. And, just as God wonders, "What is Adam going to name them?" the gaze of the cat in the bathroom asks, "Is he going to call me?"

The third layer of Derridean thinking about the animal, the accepted pathos of compassion, can be heard in the first part of *The Animal That Therefore I Am.* It is taken up again and discussed in a chapter of the dialogue with Elisabeth Roudinesco. Derrida means to substitute the *indubitable* aspect of the cogito with the *undeniable* aspect of pity. Bentham's question, *Can they suffer?*, subversively replaces the question that they pretty much all ask, Descartes, Heidegger, Levinas as well as Lacan: *Can they speak?*: "Mortality resides there, as the most radical means of thinking the finitude that we share with animals, the mortality that belongs to the very finitude of life, to the experience of compassion, . . . the anguish of this vulnerability."[22] And he adds that as humans, we can testify to this for all living things.

Today, at a moment when, he says, we have reached a critical phase in our relation to animals, pressing questions must be posed in the name of a *historial* compassion. Questions of law, ethics, politics, responsibilities, obligations—these categories need to be entirely rethought on the basis of violence toward animals. Derrida did not in fact hesitate to venture into apparently naïve practical commitments (he was, for example, the honorary president of a group working against bullfighting) that put a smirk on the faces of those who had not understood that in these marginal and trivial gestures of rupture, it was a question of a coming republic, just as it was in the past for Hugo and Michelet. I believe that for him, in the final analysis, the issue was related to the "*Come!*" of a democracy tied to the messianic experience of the *here-and-now* without which the *undeconstructable* idea of justice would remain meaningless.

Through my presentation of what Derrida sometimes names a "career in impatience," I have tried to show the continuity and discontinuity of this trajectory. It is now necessary to provide due attention to the insistence of two motifs: the motif of time and that of sacrifice. When Derrida writes, "Since time," one must commonly understand, it's been a long time, it's been such a long time that something of this order—carnophallogocentrism—has lasted, so long that animals have been forced to endure their fate. But one must also understand that the human foundation of time has depended upon this hierarchizing separation. I will nonetheless limit myself to the first and most common meaning, as it allows us to meditate on a *since forever,* on the quasi-timeless if not immemorial nature of the human relation to animals.

Men, then, would first of all be "those living creatures who have given themselves the word that enables them to speak of the animal with a single voice and to designate it as the single being that remains without a response, without a word with which to respond."[23] But where? When? And how? What is immediately striking in Derrida's work is that the radicality of his approach only ever concerns the West and its triple Judaic, Greek, Christian, and perhaps Muslim filiation: no East, no Brahmans, no Buddhism, no Schopenhauer. The deconstructive mole only digs indefinitely in the ground under Rome and Jerusalem, in the basement that ties Ionia to Iena and Freiberg to Paris. One could object to this approach that it should have gone back to the Neolithic revolution to assign an origin to this process of "an interruption that excludes" and the subjection of animals.[24] But the question of the origin seems naïve to Derrida, who, in the darkest of the supposed beginnings, only sees architraces: always already traces, perhaps even writing, less foundational than fundamental. This is therefore the case in the "scene of name calling,"[25] of that "public crying out of names" in the second story of the Genesis, a text on the basis of which he goes on, as if in a dream, occupying both places, that of the creator, as a new Jehovah, and that of the last created, another new Adam, thus bringing to an end the vulgate that imputes all the cruelty to come to the power to name.

This is a vulgate that Adorno in fact also indulged in: the dialectics of Enlightenment, he wrote to Leo Löwenthal, started with Genesis, when the power given to man to name creatures marked the beginning of a corruption of language through domination.[26] For Adorno, this was an inheritance, however impoverished, of Benjamin's meditation from the 1920s on the origin of language, a meditation that, as you will remember, Derrida evokes in *The Animal That Therefore I Am* with a great deal of precision. According to Benjamin, mourning and the sadness of nature are related to this passivity, to this stupefying wound: to have received its name and thus to find itself deprived of the power to name, to name itself, and therefore to respond.[27] Yet the Derridean Jehovah, both a severe overseer and a dreamer of chance who, *just to see,* gives his golem the

power to name, breaking entirely with the romantic tradition of
nature's melancholy that is still expressed, paradoxically, when Heidegger evokes the sadness of the animal due to its lack of world.

"Since time, since so long ago, hence since all of time and for
what remains of it to come"—to the extent that this ahistoricity,
the uchrony of the architrace, did not stop a *first* text from being
cited, it also will not keep an *epochal* meditation from being heard.
"I try to show what is specifically modern in this violence," he says,
apparently going against what he designates elsewhere as a "sacrificial structure," one to which he attributes a certain metahistoricity.
Derrida in effect shows how our contemporaries have, all while
denying their denial, continually minimized the unprecedented
proportions of the subjection of animals to which we have come.
According to another scale of time, all while maintaining the exor-
bitance of his reference to the beginning of time, he estimates signs
emerged "about two centuries ago" indicating, according to Derrida,
something very different from a historical turning point.

This goes "well beyond the animal sacrifices of the Bible or of
ancient Greece, well beyond the hecatombs (sacrifices of one hundred cattle, with all the metaphors that the expression has since been
charged with), beyond the hunting, fishing, domestication, train-
ing, or traditional exploitation of animal energy (transport, plowing,
draught animals, the horse, ox, reindeer, etc., and then the guard dog,
small-scale butchering, and then experiments on animals, etc.). It is
all too evident that in the course of the last two centuries, these traditional forms of treatment of the animal have been turned upside
down by the joint developments of zoological, ethological, biological, and genetic forms of *knowledge,* which remain inseparable from
techniques of intervention *into* their object, from the transformation
of the actual object, and from the milieu and world of their object,
namely, the living animal. This has occurred by means of farming
and regimentalization at a demographic level unknown in the past,
by means of genetic experimentation, the industrialization of what
can be called the production for consumption of animal meat, artificial insemination on a massive scale, more and more audacious
manipulations of the genome, the reduction of the animal not only

to production and overactive reproduction (hormones, genetic cross-breeding, cloning, etc.) of meat for consumption, but also of all sorts of other end products, and all of that in the service of a certain being and the putative human well-being of man."[28]

Historians of zootechnology will of course protest against a mis-interpretation of permanent continuities and ruptures, but their protests attest only to the fact that they more than anyone remain trapped in a form of denial that the philosopher refuses to be denied. One might read these pages as being close to the considerations about techno-science in Heidegger's second phase. And yet, I said to myself while reading them, here is a case where a certain pessimism is useful not only for refusing dams on the Rhine, mechanized agriculture, and the H-bomb, but for once a philosopher, with Heidegger but against him as well, represents the "hell" to which modernity has condemned animals. And if one were to suggest that Derrida is not averse to having recourse to an apocalyptic tone,[29] one would of course also have to add that the deconstruction of this "industrial, mechanical, chemical, hormonal, and genetic violence" has considerable legal and political repercussions.[30] But this would still be insufficient. For the one who notices and announces the catastrophe is the same one who, seeing himself seen naked by the little cat, mysteriously said, "*I am (following) the apocalypse itself,* that is to say, the ultimate and first event of the end, the unveiling and the verdict."[31]

On a worldwide scale, men therefore do everything possible to organize the dissimulation of this violence. And Derrida, with a curious mixture of prudence and intrepidity, evoking the "breathtaking" number of species endangered because of man, does not dismiss the qualification of "genocide." But, he adds, "One should neither abuse the figure of genocide nor too quickly consider it explained away."[32] In order for the concept to be able to seize the factual state of breeding for death, one should imagine that this annihilation of nonhuman living beings happens "through the organization and exploitation of an artificial, infernal, virtually interminable survival, in conditions that previous generations would have judged monstrous, outside of every presumed norm of a life proper to animals that are thus exterminated by means of their continued existence or even their overpopulation."[33] Tracing out an extremely transgressive parallel between tortured and slaughtered animals and the human victims of the Nazi camps, he imagines that, "in the same abattoirs," the overproduction and overgeneration of certain men would have been organized through artificial insemination, more and more numerous and well-fed men who would have been destined, in ever increasing numbers, for extermination.

One can be scandalized by this virtual evocation of the worst of the worst. As if historical reality, the proper meaning of the Extermination were not enough: in order for a reasonable equivalence to be established between the camps and slaughterhouses, one would have to have recourse to an outrageous transformation. Yet one needs to understand how Derrida works: he tears analogy away from approximation; he conjecturally modifies the historical real to give better measure of the unprecedented extent of mass birth, life, and death imposed on animals. He allows reality to be imagined, he gives a perception of the exorbitant increase in poor treatment and in the indefinite modification of individuals carried out for the sole purpose of putting them to death. This risky *variation* both places him in proximity to and distances him from certain Jewish authors of the second half of the twentieth century who were all obsessed with the "eternal Treblinka."[34] The phrase comes from Isaac Bashevis Singer, and it designates the slaughterhouses. Without a doubt, the Nazi technology for experimentation and extermination loses the precise significance given to it by its instigators and executioners when the desire for ethnic purification is replaced by the industrial production of living beings overfed and slaughtered solely for con-summation. For these authors—Adorno and Horkheimer among them—Treblinka and Auschwitz are enough to ensure their destiny as referents of the worst. The case remains, however, that something very important could be understood here concerning the *essential tie,* in agro-alimentary modernity, between overproduction, manip-ulation, and annihilation. If one adds biotechnology and genetic engineering to the picture, how can one avoid the feeling that "we are heading down the path toward . . . a world without animals . . .

by means of a devitalizing or *disanimalizing* treatment, what others would call the denaturing of animality, the production of figures of animality that are so new that they appear monstrous enough to call for a change of name."[35]

One of the most insistent hypotheses of this deconstruction with and through the animal is that a common "sacrificial structure"—though Derrida says he is not sure if this is the best way of stating it—would govern in an underground way the thinking of Descartes, Kant, Levinas, and Lacan. He does not let go of the opportunity to cite the text that can act as a first trace of this by recalling the fact that "there was also a matter of a dead animal between Cain and Abel"[36] and that God preferred the murderous shepherd to Cain, who offered his grain. He had let Adam name *to see (pour voir),* he says, and he lets Abel kill as a way of *providing (pourvoir)* him with sacrificial flesh. Does this then mean that name-giving was already equivalent to sacrificing a living being to God? The story in Genesis suggested that if Cain killed his brother, it's because he hadn't been able to offer a *sacrifice* to Jehovah. These interrogations, alongside others, would allow us to discern, despite considerable differences between eras and authors, one and the same "Judeo-Christian vein." Four philosophies of sacrificial experience are thus examined, not all necessarily treating ritual animal sacrifices. It is rather a matter of "bringing and including together, in a single embrace"[37] Kant, Heidegger, Lacan, Levinas, and even of adding Descartes to them.

So it is in an interview with Jean-Luc Nancy dating from 1989, "'Eating Well,' or the Calculation of the Subject," that we first find the strong articulation of what subtends the thought of these four cardinal thinkers. None of these thinkers will overturn the humanism proper to man without reinforcing it unbeknownst to themselves. "It is a matter of discerning a place left open, in the very structure of these discourses (which are also 'cultures') for a noncriminal putting to death. Such are the executions of ingestion, incorporation, or introjection of the corpse."[38] The operation, he says, can be real or symbolic when the "corpse" is human: some way of eating the other, some form of "cannibalism" is unsurpassable.

There is then an indestructible tie between the right to put animals to death with the goal of consuming meat and subjectity, and, more broadly with subjectivity. One must realize that this "putting to death as denegation of murder"[39] is linked to the institution of the subject: a virile schema of authority and autonomy, freedom granted man rather than woman, and woman rather than animal, the adult rather than the child, for this mastery and possession of nature implies the acceptance of sacrifice and eating flesh. In other words, the "Thou shalt not kill"—with all of its limitless consequence—has never been understood in the Judeo-Christian tradition, apparently not even by Levinas, as a "'Thou shalt not put to death the living in general.'"[40]

This point, on sacrifice, is certainly the only one where I feel I'm in disagreement with Derrida, and it is not without a certain amount of anxiety that I wish to formulate these reservations, now that he does not have the time to explain himself further. To give the background to this critique, it will be necessary to take a detour through the history of anthropology. First, one must remember that there have been and that there still are many different kinds of ritual immolation, different kinds of sacrificial functions that cannot be reduced to alimentary sacrifice: communion, of course, but also propitiation and expiation. One must then note the limitless extension Derrida attributes to the domain of sacrifice: the hyperbolic extrapolation, the metaphorization that allows him to divulge that the secret of "eating the other" cannot operate without giving short shrift to contemporary anthropological research from authors such as Jean-Pierre Vernant, Marcel Detienne, and Jean Soler, to limit ourselves to them. As a way of guarding against generalizing inductions, each of these authors insists on the singularity of the cultures and thoughts anchored in animal sacrifices, and they effectively intend to develop their analyses only through the commentaries produced within each culture.

The category of sacrifice, as it was elaborated by authors such as William Robertson Smith, Emile Durkheim, Marcel Mauss, and Ernst Cassirer—should one add Freud to them?—constitutes a catchall category that could only be constituted on the basis of an evolutionist conception of the history of religions—an evolutionism that comes from a debatable piece of evidence: according to this version of evolutionism, Christianity represents the spiritual and social accomplishment of history, and humanity develops and improves thanks to the process that consists in replacing the sacrifice offered *to* the gods with the sacrifice *of* the Christic god. Durkheim had already given the name "ascetic path," ending in Christianity, to what he thought was a wrenching away from primitive and crude forms in favor of the growth of the spirit of sacrifice. Yet Détienne rightly demonstrated the ideological presupposition that transforms the history of religions into a progress of abnegation and a recession of the contractual.

If I am taking up the "theoretical" critique formulated by the school of Jean-Pierre Vernant of the unconsidered progressivism of the founding fathers of anthropology, it is in order to show the singularity of what men in the Christian West both symbolically and truly lost all while believing they were winning interiority of intention and purity of heart: the sacred blood-tie that united them in a living community to beasts and god(s). And if we now return to the institutionally denied murder of ritual immolation, it is to suggest that Derrida's globalization, radicalization, and metaphorization of *sacrifice* do not completely escape this evolutionism, which his entire work in fact rejects. His thinking through a bloody "Epipromethean-Islamic-Judeo-Christian descendancy"[41] brings him to consider as quasi-invalid the line that divides Christianity, on the one hand, and its abolition of animal sacrifices, and Judaism and Islam, perhaps even Greek culture, on the other, which makes animal sacrifices the fundamental element of their actions.

This is why Derrida places Levinas under the same rubric as Kant and Lacan, even though Levinas the *philosopher,* despite his quasi-indifference to the death of beasts, would not really be able to think of these beasts outside of the sacrificial category to which the *practicing Jew* he is continues to obey because of dietary restrictions. For him, altars and industrial abattoirs can only have contrary meanings. I do not intend to deliver an apology for animal sacrifices here, to justify the blessed or sacred character of their cruelty, but only to affirm a conceptual unavailability. Their diversity in place and time, the plurality of their functions, their singularity, far from allowing for an understanding of contemporary practices of zootechnology and far from structuring the field of their practices into some immemorial time, seems to reserve irreducible enigmas.[42]

Yet one must indeed recognize that this contestable elevation of sacrifice to the status of a universal and secret structure is what allows Derrida, thanks to an inversion of the sign, to take up several pages by Adorno on Kant in a very gripping way. For Derrida, it is a question of showing that the valorization of *human* interiority and autonomy, those ideals of idealism and transcendentalism, not only relies on a violence committed against the sensory, but also and more importantly on a war declared on what is animal both outside of and inside man. This is a question of "cruelty," a word Derrida does not, however, use without reservation. "There can be a negotiable market price for the animal, as for every means that is incapable of becoming an end in itself, whence the virtual cruelty of this pure practical reason. Accents of cruelty already mark Kant's discourse when he speaks of the imperative necessity of *sacrificing* sensibility to moral reason. But this *sacrificial cruelty* can become so much more serious, and virtually terrible, implacable, and ferocious when it comes to the animal that some, such as Adorno, have not hesitated to denounce it as an extreme violence, even a sort of sadism."[43] Adorno will not hesitate to say that the properly *human* dignity of the autonomy that guarantees sovereignty and mastery over nature to reasonable beings is directed against animals.

And Derrida goes still further when he evokes "an act of war and a gesture of hate, an animosity,"[44] a form of violence that, like the philosopher he is commenting on, he considers to be not merely an application of techno-sciences to the animal, but "the process of humanization or of the appropriation of man by man, including its most highly developed ethical or religious forms."[45] According to this critique, Adorno does not understand Descartes, while Derrida brings Adorno back to Descartes, seeing in Kantism "a significant aggravation of 'Cartesianism' that becomes a sort of 'hatred' of the animal: 'wishing' harm to the animal." According to the two philosophers, this Kantian and more generally Idealist zoophobia is not foreign to "a Germanization or at least a fascization of the subject"[46] since there is no place left for compassion or commiseration, what with the "memory" of a resemblance or an affinity between animal and man having become abhorrent. "Then, all of a sudden, Adorno takes things much further: for an idealist system, he says, animals virtually play the same role as Jews did for the fascist system. Animals would be the Jews of the idealists, who would thus be nothing but virtual fascists."[47]

Here, we can note that Derrida and Adorno are rivals in antihumanist temerity, inheritors as they are of the *Genealogy of Morals,* even if Adorno would deny it, inheritors as well, even if both Adorno and Derrida would deny it, of the second Heidegger, and particularly of his *Nietzsche,* a book in which one finds the same "will to will" running through the entire philosophical tradition. The only difference is that they turn toward the animal suffering that is ignored or scorned by most other philosophers, starting or ending with Heidegger.

At the end of this brief debate on sacrifice, I am perplexed. Was it really necessary to *sacrifice* the comprehensive richness of monographs to a totalizing extension, to a thickening of the continuous line of what, in different forms, comes back to the identical and would thus have always already signified the worst? It is no doubt only right for anthropologists not to give lessons to their still too-philosophical predecessors and to any philosophers who adventure onto their terrain. It may be that philosophers in turn need to inform themselves more precisely about the irreducibility of diverse symbolic practices. In any case, Adorno seems to me to have most equitably unified the two perspectives when, after having opposed slaughterhouses to altars, he noted that the term "sacrifice" now only properly belonged to the vocabulary of animal experimentation. It's just, he adds, that it is as a *specimen* that one brings an animal to the laboratory while it is as a *substitute* that one brought it to the altar.[48]

"The animal that therefore I am": the diabolical ambiguity of the title given to this incisive, interminable speech that became a posthumous book is discretely unfolded in these (quasi-Borgesian) words that continue to be capable of troubling the humanism of those who gave themselves the name "men." "For I no longer know who, therefore, I am (following) or who it is I am chasing, who is following me or hunting me. Who comes before and who is after whom? . . . I no longer know how to respond to the question that compels me or asks me who I am (following) or after whom I am (following), but am so as I am running [*et suis ainsi en train de courir*]."[49]

2

The Improper

Reality of being, which man senses at the deepest level as being
alone capable of giving a reason and a meaning to his daily
activities, his moral and emotional life, his political options,
his involvement in the social and natural worlds, his practical
endeavors and his scientific achievements; the other is the reality
of non-being, awareness of which inseparably accompanies the
sense of being, since man has to live and struggle, think, believe
and above all, preserve his courage, although he can never at any
moment lose sight of the opposite certainty that he was not
present on earth in former times, that he will not always be here
in the future and that, with his inevitable disappearance from the
surface of a planet which is itself doomed to die, his labors, his
sorrows, his joys, his hopes and his works will be as if they had
never existed, since no consciousness will survive to preserve even
the memory of these ephemeral phenomena, only a few features
of which, soon to be erased from the impassive face of the earth,
will remain as already cancelled evidence that they once were, and
were as nothing.

—CLAUDE LÉVI-STRAUSS, *The Naked Man:
Mythologies,* volume 4

The philosopher who goes off in search of what is proper to man
often stops short, too quickly satisfied with abstractions and entities—essence, nature, consciousness. Scientists from any discipline
are all the more willing to make fun of his naïveté because his discourse makes claims to rigor. Either that or the philosopher simply
abdicates in the face of scientific advances and reproduces in his own
way the reductionist, even eliminationist naturalism that positivist
knowledge makes available to him. In which case he can no longer

even be a philosopher, for he is only vulgarizing by acquiescing to fatalistic determinism. This presents a double difficulty: how can one both avoid using sophisticated words and theoretical or metaphysical concepts without showing a lack of respect for the terrible adventure of events and annihilations we call history? How can one sustain a philosophical project without rehashing and refounding the metaphysical tradition of the human exception from which Heidegger himself, that wonderful deconstructor of "the reasonable animal," was unable to escape?[1] To the extent that the unrelenting pursuit of definition and segregation remains haunted by the quest for this proper to man that in the final analysis always gives itself as *presence,* one must indeed accept the fact that at the beginning of the twenty-first century, we must think of the being of man as something both tragic and unrepresentable: we are surrounded by the distant past of our species, the recent past of our historicity, and the uncertain future of our humanity, *absences* that make affirmations of specificity and efforts at determination ridiculous.

When Joseph de Maistre on the one hand and Marx on the other said they saw man nowhere, but saw only singular and concrete men, whether because of their cultural allegiances or their social conditions, they did not radically invalidate the traditional teachings of Pauline, Cartesian, and Kantian humanism according to which men, as different as they may be in space and in time, are all a part of humanity to the extent that they form an empire within the empire of the living. They were only proposing an empirical, synchronic, and diachronic observation of the irreducible diversity of peoples and of conditions. Discoveries of these last several years, on the other hand, bearing on the origin of *Homo sapiens,* genetics, and the abilities of the great apes have certainly begun to threaten the concept of humanity, since man is now only a species of the genus *Homo.* How Linné, who was the first to imagine this offensive inclusion— one rejected by Buffon—could reconcile it with the Christian faith is actually something very difficult to understand.[2]

Scientific research and the writing of a postmodern and resolutely anti-metaphysical philosophy have rightly ruined the humanist and always still secretly creationist faith we have in the unique character of human history at its implicit and self-righteous foundations.[3] A *decision* must nonetheless be firmly maintained, one that forces us to keep two heterogeneous interrogations apart: that of the origin of man and that of the meaning of the human. To state this in other terms, one cannot allow the intersections of research from paleo-anthropologists and primatologists, or discoveries in molecular biology and in genetics to destroy *without remains* the affirmation of the rupture constituted by anthropological singularity. And it is therefore not certain that we can do without recourse to philosophical tradition.

To cite a currently raging debate, when the argument of a primatologist attributes a moral sense to animals and makes this the basis of human altruism,[4] one must begin with a call to order: deducing what must be from what is, the deontological from the ontological, is a method that is, of course, not prohibited—Spinoza gave it a grandiose and hard-to-refute status—but, at least at first, should not be taken for granted. For before attributing some kind of moral sense to certain animals or affirming that intuitions and ethical behavior in human beings *naturally* derive from evolution, one would have to reach an agreement as to the meaning of "moral sense," an ambiguous expression laden with anthropomorphism. It is premature to pronounce a verdict solely on the basis of a vague consensus as to what the common denominator baptized "altruism" might be. But one wonders more particularly what authority could legitimately decide between continuity and discontinuity. In which discipline and according to which system of validation could one find the criterion that would allow us to judge if a form of animal or human behavior is related to morality or only to a *natural* altruism? Besides certain historical approaches, I see hardly anything but philosophical reflection, insofar as it is nourished by the critical reexamination of its own tradition, as capable of effectively reflecting on this subject. Neurobiological or ethological knowledge and the ethnological, psychological, and sociological disciplines can contribute to the construction of a science of social customs, to the description and anchoring of what is called a "habitus" or an "ethos" in certain processes. Yet no one will ever obtain from these forms of knowledge the authorization to decide that the fact of crossing over such and such a limit in abnegation or resistance stems from the instinctual conservation of one's own or from profitable exchange rather than from an incomprehensible self-sacrifice without compensation. "Within the limits of your field alone one does not know what it means to 'evaluate' or 'create a norm,'" Paul Ricoeur brilliantly responded to Jean-Pierre Changeux.[5] And this warning remains true even if one takes into account what Patrick Tort calls the "reverse effect of evolution": Darwin in effect showed that at a moment of evolution, a reversal takes place, since civilized men annul the effects of natural selection by protecting the most fragile individuals.[6]

Though I recognize my debt to Ricoeur, the response I will propose to the naturalist antihumanism that intones the "end of the human exception" will dispense with principles.[7] An ethics and a politics founded on the affirmation of the singularity of humankind, and thus on its unity, on the effective respect for the dignity of each of those who are part of humanity, and on the claim for an uncompromising fraternity among all beings who come from a man and a woman, or even from a man or a woman, far from being invalidated by this metaphysical neutrality, find themselves reinforced by it. By trying to maintain a disillusioned approach to human reality, one commits oneself to cease vainly delighting in "values" and invoking "spirit." Sobriety and prudence bring us, in effect, to avoid this panic about our identity, a panic that throws us without precaution onto the raft of ethics, free will, and the Other. The little bit of *sense* that remains at the end of this trial inflicted on humanist consensus forms a kernel that establishes an authority that is all the more demanding because the void has been carved out in it, and a tie that is all the more inestimable because it is fragile. It is at the end of this purging that we must *decide* that the *signification of the human* does not allow itself to be deciphered solely from knowledge of the origin of humanity and its biological reality. A materialist approach must sustain the minimal rigor that consists in a method adequate to its object, must not succumb to physicalist reductionisms and eliminationisms, must not confuse facts with norms, nature with history, and must not flatten the tortured and often unpredictable texture of the relations of men with one another.

The fact remains that if we recall the succession of immemorial and irrefutable signs of anthropological difference and note the retreat into which advances in the life sciences have forced sacrosanct human difference, one can't help but laugh. Must we begin by giving a list of these supposed capacities? Yes, probably, and in a jumble like Prévert would sometimes do, without putting them in any particular order. At the very beginning, man was "created in God's likeness." Then Aristotle will say, at the beginning of book 1 of the *Politics,* that man's being consists in "having" language and reason. But before that, the Pre-Socratic philosopher Anaxagoras had made the point that man thinks because he has hands. Over the course of time, it was a question of vertical posture, fire, writing, agriculture, mathematics, philosophy, of course, freedom, and therefore morality, perfectibility, the capacity for imitation, anticipation of death, work, neurosis, the ability to lie, social debate, sharing food, art, laughter, inhumation . . . Research in genetics, paleoanthropology, primatology, and zoology will have pulverized the majority of these certainties and made this pretentious emulation and proof of incomparable competence look ridiculous. The chimpanzee's language, the uncapping of milk bottles by English titmice, the gibbon's monogamy, the ant's altruism, and the praying mantis's cruelty leave us speechless. For unless we allow philosophical reflection to morph into rhetorical pompousness, we can now no longer oppose nature to culture, the innate to the acquired, man to animal.[8] The dialectical setting into interaction of these antinomies is no longer capable of accounting for the doing and being of men: everything that is afoot and being discovered today invites us to see complacent abstraction in these couples whose very rifts have become reassuring. Thus, for example, the Hegelian-Marxist conception of work as what is proper to man often renews the most insistent and gratifying motifs in modern philosophy: the positive negativity exerted by subjectivity on the given.

It will not suffice however to note the fragility of these criteria; one must also show their eminently harmful character. In the hesitation into which the future, past, and present state of our knowledge and power has led us, is it not most urgent, and most prudent, to settle on a minimal declaration and a modest remark? In this case, and although the perspective of reproductive cloning probably makes such a determination provisional, we will say that a human being is a being born of the natural or artificially provoked union of a woman and a man: a generous and simplistic criterion, like the *jus soli*. This zero degree of definition allows us not to make the criminal mistake that would lead us to exclude from humanity the one or the ones who do not conform to a decisive sign: "savages" (who lack rationality or historicity), criminals (who lack "humanity"), the mentally handicapped (who lack liberty and perfectibility), weakened elderly people, even infants (who are lacking in all the characteristics that constitute what is properly human).

What allows us to recognize a man? The question is indecent, for everyone knows right away "if this is a man."[9] And anyone who does not immediately recognize their fellow man has prejudices and has decided that certain ethnic groups, certain cultures, and certain individuals foreign to their standards should not have the right to existence or to social visibility. Yet the criminal rejection of certain beings outside of humanity can operate in more surreptitious ways, relying quite precisely on those criteria endlessly elaborated by the speculations of metaphysics and by certain studies in the life sciences, sometimes even by certain social sciences. For one cannot base oneself on certain criteria of humanity without also excluding, whether one wants to or not, whether one knows it or not, those who in some way vary from the definition claiming to define human difference: the definition in this case functions as a norm and as an exclusion. To limit oneself as much as is possible, without paradox or provocation, to a negative anthropology, to affirm the fact that man is a being who neither can nor must be defined thus seems to be the only appropriate way of behaving: ethically, politically, and scientifically. This will be the perspective of this study, even if, to avoid any complacency with the emphatic ontological recuperation by the "void," I may propose certain characteristics by which it would seem that we can recognize human difference.

Instead of Genesis and its elaboration of how God decided to "make man in our image, after our likeness,"[10] a sentence that gives us too much to think about, the chorus from *Antigone* comes to mind—

or at least to the minds of those who continue to listen to the Greek origin of Western culture.[11] The text that Sophocles places into the mouths of the old wise men terrified by the audacity of this young woman who is disobedient to the point of being willing to die was inscribed by Heidegger into his philosophical work. And because this translation makes these verses from Sophocles excessively Heideggerian, it allows us to hear them from the furthest distance and in closest proximity to our uncertain humanity.

> Manifold is the uncanny, yet nothing
> uncannier than man bestirs itself, rising up beyond him.
> He fares forth upon the foaming tide
> amid winter's southerly tempest
> and cruises through the summits
> of the raging, clefted swells.
> The noblest of gods as well, the earth,
> the indestructibly untiring, he wearies,
> overturning her from year to year,
> driving the plows this way and that
> with his steeds.
>
> Even the lightly gliding flock of birds
> he snares, and he hunts
> the best folk of the wilderness
> and the brood whose home is the sea,
> the man who studies wherever he goes.
>
> With ruses he overwhelms the beast
> that spends its nights on mountains and roams,
> and clasping with wood
> the rough-manned neck of the steed
> and the unvanquished bull
> he forces them into the yoke.
>
> Into the sounding of the word, as well,
> and into wind-swift all-understanding
> he found his way, and into the mettle

to rule over cities.
He has considered, too, how he might flee
exposure to the arrows
of unpropitious weather and its frosts.

Everywhere trying out, underway; untried, with no way out
he comes to Nothing.
A single onslaught, death, he was unable
ever to resist by any flight,
even if in the face of dire illness
deft escape should be granted him.

Clever indeed, for he masters
skill's devices beyond expectation,
now he falls prey to wickedness,
yet again valor succeeds for him.
Between the ordinance of the earth and the
Gods' sworn dispensation [*Fug*] he fares.
Rising high over the site, losing the site
is he for whom what is not, is, always,
for the sake of daring.

Let him not become a companion at my hearth,
nor let my knowing share the delusions
of the one who works such deeds.[12]

Deinos: that which inspires fear and strikes the imagination. Man appears as what is most disquieting: that exorbitant being that does violence and oversteps limits. These stanzas seem to recapitulate prophetically the characteristics of anthropological difference: domination over nature, many technical apparatuses, politics, death recognized as inevitable, good and evil, ambivalence, absolute danger. That which the Greeks named *hubris,* or "excessiveness," though the word does not appear in the text. If what the tragedy says is capable of illuminating a meditation on human singularity, it's because everything about the difficulty of stating what and who man is can be found in it. Hans Jonas writes of the chorus in *Antigone,* saying that this awestruck homage to man's powers tells of his violent and violating irruption into the cosmic order and places mastery and dominion over the waves, the earth, the dizzied birds, the fish populating the sea, the horse with its thick mane and the tireless bull into equilibrium with respect for the state's laws and humility before death: a no doubt more ecological and political and certainly less ontological way of understanding the lesson.[13] He writes that nature could not take any greater risk than allowing man to be born. This, then, was one of the first ways that man was presented to men.

Compared to this poetic statement, how much less tragic and disquieting does the famous passage from book 1 of the *Politics* appear, where Aristotle declares what is proper to man in a way that, in turn, cannot not seem to us any less inaugural since we have not emancipated ourselves intellectually from this tradition even though contemporary knowledge seems to take us further and further away from it with vertiginous speed. Here then is that major premise of all metaphysics—and perhaps of any politics to come. "Now, that man is more of a political animal [*politikon zōon*] than bees or any other gregarious animals is evident. . . . [M]an is the only animal who has the gift of speech. And whereas mere voice [*phonē*] is but an indication of pleasure or pain, and is therefore found in other animals (for their nature attains to the perception of pleasure and pain and the intimation of them to one another, and no further), the power of speech [*logos*] is intended to set forth the expedient and inexpedient, and therefore likewise the just and the unjust. And it is a characteristic [*idion*] of man that he alone has any sense of good and evil, of just and unjust, and the like, and the association of living beings who have this sense makes a family and a state."[14] Because of its strong articulation of language and politics—activities that can exist only together—this argument seems so irrefutable that no one has ever truly been able to surpass it by stating a more decisive given criterion of humanity. In fact, the Sophists proposed a representation of man that is fairly close to this one. Plato in effect

has the Sophist Protagoras recount how after Epimetheus wasted all
his available gifts on animals, Prometheus discovered that man was
lacking in all the abilities indispensable to his survival.[15] In addition
to language and fire, he therefore also gave them the art of politics
and the "shamefulness" that provide his singularity.[16] It nonetheless
remains the case that it is the very notion of a discriminating characteristic that poses a problem now that the diversity of man is
becoming increasingly clear, a diversity that has always been passed
off as inequality, and now that, in addition, long ignored animal
capacities are revealed, even if they were intuited in the fables and
extraordinary stories transmitted by Plutarch and Pliny the Elder,
which survived all the way through to Montaigne in his "Apologie
of Raymond Sebond."[17]

There is also the materialist tradition, which refuses to allow for
man to puff himself up at the thought of man, and the cynical tradition illustrated by Diogenes' famous story of bringing a plucked
chicken to the academy, declaring, "Here is man according to
Plato."[18] The philosopher had dared to propose a highly risky definition: a biped without feathers! It is nonetheless in one of the very
same Plato's dialogues, *The Statesman,* that we encounter a certain
"Young Socrates."[19] During a discussion on how divisions, or classifications, should be made, Young Socrates notes that common
opinion traces a dividing line between man and all other animals,
which is doubly mistaken: first of all, there is the methodological
weakness of hastily incorporating the species into the genus; the
second mistake is a moral one and consists in commonly using a separation that subjectivizes and annihilates the use of dichotomies—
as a result, it does not obtain real classifications and displays only
the self-glorification of the classifying subject who, full of himself,
places himself outside all other living beings.

When the Greeks or Hellenics, for example, designate the majority of all other men as "barbarians," they do not understand that
one single name does not constitute one single genus—and they
incorrectly articulate the one with the multiple. This logical mistake
has its origin in the belief in the superiority of the Greek language:
this conviction leads to the occultation of real differences to the

benefit of a historical difference that abusively separates the same from the same, in this case the Greeks from the others. One must nonetheless note, says the interlocutor, that any nation would make the same mistake, which can be explained by the presence of an auto-centered subject acting as the operator of the division. Incapable of cutting up reality as a good butcher cuts up meat, this subject places value, or the greatest ontological density, on the side of the one who is speaking. Even more than that, any animal that may have the capacity to reason—a crane, for example—would make the same mistake: it would divide living beings into cranes and all the others taken in one block, indistinctly, in one and the same genus. This aberrant partition resides in effect in the *logos,* in the capacity to reason and to speak, and in the auto-veneration that inheres in the one who speaks: the subject plants himself and drapes himself in the unicity of his species, and the self-consciousness of the classifier brings him to reject the confused mass of all the others onto the exterior. It is therefore a narcissistic desire that causes the logical mistake. The function of the allegory of the crane is to show that the human in no way offers a stable figure. For Plato, in fact, there is nothing proper to man: only souls that are incarnated in men or in animals according to their degree of spirituality.[20] Yet this apology of the crane allows us to understand more generally and more radically that this age-old repetition of an auto-proclamation testifies to self-complacency—one we will certainly not call a "speciesism": it never stopped men from treating other men in the most horrible ways.

Gauguin called the painting he considered his artistic testament *Where Do We Come From? What Are We? Where Are We Going?* It could be that this painting and its caption testify to our indetermination with as much eloquence as anything written on the ontological enigma that man is for man. The innocent and incredulous faces of the characters in the painting and these three pressing questions suggest only a question addressed to humans plunged into the double uncertainty of their provenance and of their destination, the uncertainty that bears on the direction and meaning of their existence as individuals and as humankind. So what is it that we are?

At the beginning of the second millennium, when we look at this painting and read these words within it, we no longer think only of birth and death or of the mysterious beginnings and unpredictable future of humanity. For we know, thanks to knowledge that is being constantly confirmed, Darwin was right about our ascendancy, about the hazardous emergence of hominization, which has nothing to do with the creation of a being placed outside all other living beings. And we certainly suspect that such a being is not destined to personal immortality. The experience of finitude and of abandonment is effectively disturbed by genealogical and now also genetic knowledge that, informing us about both the past and the present of the species and the individual, leaves us in the uncertainty of tomorrows that are nonetheless already written: death and reproduction, the disappearance of phenotype, somatic ipseity with the potential transmission of the genotype, and that is all.

A hundred years earlier, Kant had already formulated similar questions, but for him there were four of them: "1. What can I know? 2. What ought I to do? 3. What may I hope? 4. What is man?"[21] Kant maintained that the last question was the most important. This enumeration encapsulates in a lapidary manner all of Kant's works in a kind of tetralogy. In his two *Critiques, Religion within the Limits of Reason Alone* and *Anthropology,* the philosopher thought he had resolved these enigmas. Man cannot know absolute reality, but can base himself on science; he must believe in freedom to obtain autonomous will, which is what morality is; he is permitted to hope in a God, yet thought of this God must remain contained within the limits of reason alone. The human figure that emerges from these three lines of knowledge, duty, and belief should have been enough. Unfortunately, the *Anthropology,* with its positively articulated description of *what* men are, a book where Kant repeats the worst racist, misogynist, and normalizing clichés, spoils the admirable order in which one nonetheless found the affirmation that man is not only a phenomenon. A footnote from this work should nonetheless be mentioned here. Though Kant does not explicitly ask himself where we come from, he does consider the possibility that a second era of great revolutions in nature will be followed by a third, "when an ourang-utan or a chimpanzee develops the organs used for walking, handling objects, and speaking into the structure of a human being, whose innermost part contains an organ for the use of the understanding and which developed gradually through social culture."[22] This note indirectly confirms that it is the freedom of the moral subject that grounds dignity as what is proper to man, and not articulated language.

In the end, the interrogation into what man is comes not so much from descriptive knowledge as from the following political and techno-biological question: what have we done to man and what are we going to do with him? The two moments at the source of these interpellations have names, if one dares to "philosophize with a hammer": Nazism and cloning. Of course, in spite of the Nazi history of genetics and human experimentation, no analogy should be inconsiderately established between these two ways of handling life and death. But how can one avoid first of all acknowledging that most *definitions* of man or humanity have lost their meaning since the Nazis became a racist state and attempted, with a certain degree of success, to exterminate men they held to be subhuman: confronted with this proclaimed and actualized intention, beautiful humanist and democratic ideals revealed their impotence and hypocrisy.

This despair was the backdrop for Emmanuel Levinas's decision to entitle one of his books *Humanism of the Other,* where he implicitly recognizes an essential link between metaphysics, and even Kantian critique, and the technically perpetrated genocide. After the genocide, no knowledge of living human beings can be exonerated from the history of men. Positivists of all schools and in all disciplines blithely reassure themselves, yet they are actually criminally mistaken when they situate our origin only in the natural order of animality and thus neglect to make it begin again, on the historical level, in Auschwitz and its crimes against humanity, which—collateral effects!—inflicted *us* with narcissistic wounds far worse than heliocentrism, evolutionism, and psychoanalysis combined.

And if, secondly, we were now once again to ask ourselves where we are going and toward what, and what we many hope for, transgenesis and reproductive cloning, which have now become inevitable,

must be addressed along with the programmed though provision-
ally prohibited abolition of the categories of the same and other
that have, up until now, been considered foundational for all human
thinking and action. It is now no longer a question of defining man
but of changing him, to the benefit of things that are purely possible
and that have no other reference beyond *our* power to bring them
about, to work not toward the emergence of a new humanity but
toward the production of beings other than humans. Yet in order to
speak of a being other than man, we would have to have defined
man, something which, as we have seen, must be avoided at all costs
for both scientific and ethical reasons. All of our points of reference
seem to escape us after National Socialism and in the era of genetic
engineering. Just try to pronounce upon the nature of man or the
signification of the human without trembling: we are undone at the
very heart of our ascendancy and our posterity.

Philosophy, in spite of the unavoidable reference I made when I
cited Paul Riceour's response to Jean-Pierre Changeux, seems too
disparate and philosophers too involved in permanent mutual destitution for us, in the depths of our tumult about human identity, to be able to find in this discipline the consensual and lasting
anchoring that we might otherwise expect from it. Shall we paint
a picture of these disagreements? Empiricism, skepticism, materialism, and existentialism have always opposed the innatist—and
a-priorist—school that affirms that there is something universal in
man that precedes any experience, and they refuse the idea of an
essence or of a predetermined human nature. Already at the Greek
origins of philosophy, the partisans of the innate fought with those
who see in every man the result of the interaction between the given
and the constructed. The paradox of our contemporary debate is
that the confrontation between the innate and the acquired, in other
words, between the genetic and the epigenetic, is played out in new
terms, if not quite in reverse order, now that the conflict opposes
innatists, determinists who believe that "everything is genetic," and
empiricists, who accentuate the constructive and contingent nature
of sociality.

Man is a chameleon, for it befalls him "to have what he chooses, to be what he wills to be," as Giovanni Pico della Mirandola wrote with jubilation. "We have given you, Oh Adam, no visage proper to yourself, nor any endowment properly your own, in order that whatever place, whatever form, whatever gifts you may, with premeditation, select, these same you may have and possess through your own judgment and decision. The nature of all other creatures is defined and restricted within laws which We have laid down; you, by contrast, impeded by no such restrictions, may, by your own free will, to whose custody We have assigned you, trace for yourself the lineaments of your own nature. . . . in order that you may, as the free and proud shaper of your own being, fashion yourself in the form you may prefer."[23] Rousseau will in turn ask, "Here is as far as man can go, and no further?"[24] Those who are called existentialists will also lay claim to this antinaturalist current up to a certain point. Yet if Heidegger's thought is to be catalogued under this title, it is difficult to imagine how this philosopher could be placed in the same category as Sartre, given the fact that their respective conceptions of humanism are radically opposed in *Existentialism Is a Humanism* and the *Letter on Humanism*.[25] The fact that man is haunted by the void, an argument that the Frenchman inherited from the German, led each of them down opposite paths.

But the greatest dispersion comes no doubt from the division that emerged in the twentieth century between, on the one hand, the so-called continental philosophy of the great metaphysical tradition and its deconstruction and, on the other hand, Anglo-Saxon philosophy, known as analytic philosophy: the divide is deep and the mutual contestation is ferocious. One need only remember the way Carnap, a philosopher in the Vienna Circle, thought he had pulverized several sequences in a Heideggerian text in which it was precisely a question of the relation of man to speech and to nonbeing: one sees in it the nonnegotiable violence of a disagreement.[26] The situation is even more disturbing when one discovers the line that splits analytic philosophy itself between a philosophy of mind and language, illustrated by Wittgenstein, and a naturalist (monist, eliminationist) vein that avoids even so much as a theory of emergence. What might one add to speak of the relation each of the orientations has with psychoanalysis, which seems still today to constitute, in the contemporary anthropological maelstrom, an articulate, stable discourse on the human that is relatively capable of an aggiornamento?

Just before this intolerant division began, one that at least bears witness to the vitality of philosophy and to the fact that it is very difficult to exploit it to one's own ends, Nietzsche, a figure who is brazenly ignored by analytic philosophers, appeared as the one who, concerning man, "that bloodless abstraction, that fiction,"[27] rigorously came to terms with the Darwinian revolution. In order to take proper measure of this Nietszchean moment, one must find a way to seize the figure of the *Übermensch* and the concept of the will to power in a nonbiological way.

Though he expresses his reservations several times,[28] notably considering the struggle for life as a unilateral representation in which he sees merely an exception to the great waste of the will to power, and even criticizes the concepts of the individual and of the species,[29] Nietzsche draws in part on the theory of evolution to liquidate the humanist consolations of theology, metaphysics, and morality. He does not hesitate to praise Darwinism as "the last great philosophical movement."[30] He finds a figure for his skepticism, and even of his conception of the eternal return, in the double motif of the ape as an ancestor of man and of man as "the ape of God."[31] He cites the possibility, no doubt little in keeping with the letter of Darwinism yet appropriate for the idea of the eternal return, of a "circular orbit of humanity . . . a stage in the evolution of a certain species of animal of limited duration." In such a way, he writes, "that man has emerged from the ape and will return to the ape, while there will be no one present to take any sort of interest in this strange cosmic conclusion."[32] What is most remarkable is that Nietzsche immediately understood the strong support the contingency of Darwinian evolution could bring to his own critique of teleology. "Possibly the ant in the forest is quite as firmly convinced that it is the aim and purpose of the existence of the forest, just as we are convinced in our imaginations (almost unconsciously) that the destruction of mankind involves the destruction of the world."[33] And elsewhere he writes of "the vanity that man is the great secret objective of animal evolution. Man is absolutely not the crown of creation: every creature stands beside him at the same stage of perfection."[34] Utterly pagan humility of a cry that says "Us unique in the world, ah!" a warning that should have made Bergsonism and Teilhardism improbable, a premonition, in many of its textual moments, of what today appears as the possibly specific difference of the human being, when he writes that "man is the animal whose proper characteristic is still undetermined."[35]

"The symbolic animal": this is how Cassirer presents the rational animal in an impressive study in transcendental anthropology that elucidates the formal conditions that make human experience possible.[36] He intends to add to the a priori forms of sensibility and to the Kantian categories of understanding the linguistic a prioris that produce symbols. Heidegger questioned this return to Kant, deeming it still too concentrated on the theory of knowledge and opposed to it the reading he gives of the *Critique of Pure Reason* on the basis of the experience of the temporality of *Dasein,* in other words of human reality.[37] It is important to cite this considerable dispute of the late 1920s, because in this debate, Cassirer no doubt both refined and enriched extant discourse on man. But it is Heidegger who, haunted by finitude and the constitutive void of human reality, seems in spite of it all to come closest to negative anthropology, whose noble demand could have carried the day if his definition of *Dasein,* of "being-for-death," hadn't led him to establish an abyss between man and animal that makes him blind to the living.

Lévi-Strauss's structural anthropology carefully avoided all of the metaphysical pitfalls that snag, more or less triumphantly, so many philosophers. And yet he begins by refusing a methodology that would rely on primatology and paleoanthropology to reconstruct a so-called natural state of man. In *The Elementary Structures of Kinship,* the ethnographer's work opens with an absolutely original position on the relation between nature and culture.[38] On the side of nature, one finds instinctive regulations, spontaneity, and universality. On the side of culture, one finds obligatory and relative rules. Lévi-Strauss maintains the affirmation of both a discontinuity and an articulation between nature and culture. This is because the prohibition of incest, which does not stem from reproduction without at the same time being related to alliance, which imposes itself as a norm and yet presents the characteristic of universality, attests to the double belonging of the human fact and keeps us from constituting humanity as a separate order. The connection of the instinctual and the social set into place by symbolic and a priori structures concerns not only the exchange in women, but also that of words and of possessions and services, three systems of reciprocity among which we therefore discover a homology.

Beyond the heterogeneity of cultures and the quasi-untranslatability between them, there seems to be a properly human, unconscious universal, a kind of logical operator that allows different societies to affect, each in its own way, classifications and categorizations. In his final works, Lévi-Strauss will distance himself from the quasi-mathematical character that he had attributed to this fundamental invariant, to this symbolic activity, and to these universal forms for the functioning of the human mind. But his hypothesis of a *human mind* remains a radical idea, a *nature never given to itself,* impossible to represent, a pure condition of possibility of the attribution of meaning: impossible to substantiate, and even less to be used as a way of legitimating a psychological or social constraint.

If it is important to insist on the function of the pure conditions of possibility that are represented by symbolic forms, this is because many use structural anthropology to restore, over the ruins of religion and metaphysics, a constraining order. A symbolic operator and a process of symbolization do not form a symbolic order that could be presented as a condition sine qua non for hominization or humanization, while *desymbolization* is, sometimes abusively, identified and stigmatized.[39] Against those who, when faced with certain societal proposals, claim the authority to pronounce upon the imminence of an escape from humanity, one must keep the theoretical observation of the symbolic from systematically occupying the vacant place of the ethical injunction of divine commandment.

These reservations also hold true for the Lacanian signifier, that name-of-the-father that opens to the symbolic order in so far as this order differentiates itself from the imaginary and the real. Lacan's work is no more apt than is Lévi-Strauss's (and there is no reason here to note the difference between an order with a subject and an order without a subject) to justify ideologies of resistance to change, for they have no objective beyond the theorization of constitutive human actions. To take this transcendental for a transcendent, to take these profound structures for norms to which we have a right when confronted with techno-scientific progress and institutional mutations, to decry the dangers of barbarity or psychosis is to confuse the political, the juridical, and the clinical. The ethico-political uses of the symbolic order are therefore no less equivocal than the uses of nature, whenever one intends to inscribe the essence of man into it in an authoritarian manner.[40]

A sense of uneasiness does now persist, in relation to something like the *Law:* an imperious and laconic demand, like the statue of the Commendatore. Can we allow ourselves to slight the notion of the limit? What obliges us (and note that I did not write *what might oblige us*) not passively to say yes to any social initiative, to any techno-scientific progress, under the pretext that it is new? And at the same time, as we wonder about what measures the limit and about the obligation to watch over that measure, how can we work toward avoiding the renewal of Revelation, metaphysics, and the denial of immanence?

Research in ethology has seriously called into question the possibility of attributing the symbolic function only to humanity. In the conclusion to *The Naked Man,* Claude Lévi-Strauss acknowledges that animals have symbolic behavior, but he suggests that the disproportion between their weak ability to symbolize and their great physical power explains why we do not sufficiently emphasize this characteristic common to animality and humanity. This is the opposite of Cassirer who, when he proposes his theory of man as a symbolic animal, cites the work of Uexküll, Koehler, and Yerkes, but only as a way of showing what is proper to human symbolization.

According to Cassirer, human symbolization does not limit itself to signs and functions on the basis of symbols capable of opening up to a specific modality of being, to an autonomous world.

The echoes of ethology that disconcert those who maintain metaphysical humanism resonated into the writings of Husserl and Merleau-Ponty. Meditating on research by Lorenz, Merleau-Ponty makes his way to the enigmatic observation of an animal symbolism that he understands as a "preculture." Through Lorenz he effectively discovers in instinct a primordial activity "without object . . . which is not primitively the position of an end,"[41] as is attested by the gesticulations, ceremonials, monstrations, and displays of presence in which "doing" is replaced by "being seen." They are characteristic of each species and manifest as many styles. Certain instinctive activities, in fact, are exerted merely for pleasure and are referenced on "the inactual." This indicates that instinct is of a sacred and absolute nature, as if the animal wanted and at the same time did not want his object. Instinct is both "in itself and turned towards the object, it is both an inertia and a hallucinatory, oneiric behavior, capable of making a world and of picking up any object of the world."[42]

With these purposeless gestures and the derailing of instinct, so-called cultural behavior appears in the symbolic activities of which animals show themselves capable. These minimal or mimed actions, these substitutes for effective action are going to transform into activities that are incomprehensible in the context of conditioning and that function as *resonances.* Neither the mechanistic explanation nor the finalist interpretation can account for what must indeed be called "animal culture."[43] Merleau-Ponty thus concludes that "we no longer see where behavior begins and where mind ends."[44] The architecture of symbols the animal constructs does indeed confirm the existence of a preculture, as Uexküll, Lorenz's teacher, had maintained. When one follows along the unbroken line that begins with the planned-out and quasi-mechanic living beings, continues through the living beings that plan themselves out but whose instincts have very little or no freedom, and concludes with the animal that seems to have no design, so much is its instinct capable of functioning without purpose, what do we see if not an animal who rises toward an *Umwelt*, an environment and a milieu of events that "opens on a temporal and spatial field,"[45] less and less oriented toward a goal and consisting more and more in the interpretation of symbols and in unheard-of relations?

Who then should we *believe?* Montaigne, who said that there is sometimes a greater difference between one man and another than between an animal and a man,[46] or Descartes, who made the answering word the criterion of the human, even refusing to exclude from it the mute and the insane?[47] There is something both unavoidable and undecidable in this alternative that has been repeated since the beginning of Western history and that has not stopped opposing us to one another. Leaving aside the provocative Derridean idea of a "repeatedly folded frontier"[48]—here, in a kind of urgency, I must do so—I will not be able to avoid the oft-rehashed criterion of a specifically human language.[49] For however far the work of primatologists may lead us in their research on communication with the great apes and their abilities to categorize, we run the risk of *asinanity* (*bêtise*)[50] if we insist on denying that men express themselves and communicate differently than the most intelligent and loquacious of animals. There is a double articulation that allows us to characterize this properly linguistic aspect, the first assembling minimal unities, monemes that even when isolated have form and meaning and are commutable, while the second bears on the commutation of distinct minimal unities with a phonetic form, or phonemes.

Onto this deep structure is added a capacity lacking in non-human primates, as naturalist philosophers themselves recognize in their theorizations of convergent research in biology, experimental psychology, neurophysiology, and cognitive ethology. This capacity is declarative language, speech that is produced to give information, or ostensive language with the function of showing someone else an object, not to obtain it but only to have it shown. It is also continuously shared experience, insofar as it mobilizes a conjoined attention. It is also conversational language, which implies intersubjectivity, the ability to represent for myself what the other represents for him- or herself, his or her mental states in their difference from mine, and the capacity to take this difference into account.[51]

But to this tableau, one should add the performative capacity because it resonates with the political theme of this book. In rhetoric, a performative utterance designates an affirmation that simultaneously constitutes the act to which it refers; it is a *Fiat!,* a "Let this be!" It brings this speech that is an act into the order of things and therefore has the capacity to act upon the real and to transform it by the very fact of its being pronounced. This is why when we declare ourselves "humankind," we effectively separate ourselves as if by oath, historically and politically; we free ourselves, *knowingly,* from the fact of our belonging to a species. As Aristotle showed,[52] one can paradoxically say that what animals are lacking in the final analysis is everything that is related to *doxa,* to belief, persuasion, adhesion, and therefore to rhetoric. If they may benefit from the use of a certain *logos,* they will never have access to what Latin called *oratio,* speech, to the register where the logical and the linguistic are articulated to constitute the public and human space of deliberation. In fact, it is the ethico-rhetorical more than the rational that constitutes the specificity of the human. And we can all agree that deeming this, so close to the thought of the Sophists, what is proper to man has nothing metaphysical about it!

In this same perspective and with a slight shift in emphasis, one can wonder whether it is not in metaphorical power that the difference may be situated. "*Ein Hund/der stirbt/und der Weiss/dass er stirbt/wie ein Hund/und der sagen kann/dass er Weiss/dass er stirbt/wie ein Hund/ist ein Mensch:* A dog that is dying and that knows that he's dying like a dog and that can say that he knows that he's dying like a dog is a man."[53] The use of metaphor and tragic experience recapitulate simultaneously the singular relation of men to other men, to the referent, to animals, and to the world. And this would therefore perhaps constitute that signification of the human that I refuse, for ethical and historical reasons, to abandon to positivist liquidation.

Yet we must also address this question from the perspective of anthropology. Convinced by the latest results of primatology and the synthetic theory of evolution, Maurice Godelier unhesitatingly attributes to primates living in multi-male and multi-female groups the imaginary, the symbolic, and the capacity to transmit.[54] In the absence of articulated language, primates are able to use corporeal and environmental signs that they interpret and which make sense to them and to others: schemas (percepts and semiconcepts) that organize action by allowing for a representation of the virtual. Taking up a description from Christophe Boetsch on the transmission of nut-cracking with a stone,[55] he renders the observation more precise on the basis of the observations of another primatologist.[56] The mother will occasionally slow her gesture down as a way to teach it better, which indicates that she represents her own gesture to herself enough to present it as a model to be imitated, that she therefore transforms an ordinary gesture into an exemplary one.

The anthropologist does, however, argue that the peacemaking behavior analyzed by Frans de Waal shows, contrary to primatologists' interpretations, that primates living in groups cannot modify the global structure of the relations proper to their species, while humans, through their language, have the capacity to effectuate two operations.[57] The first consists in the fact of looking for an explanation at the origin of things and of oneself; I will only mention that aptitude, because emphasizing it might encourage a return to the religious and metaphysical—and in the end to too great a valorization of the theoretical, an overly facile renewal, in other words, of the human exception. The second operation, on the other hand, consists in giving oneself a global representation of the organizing principles of society as a way of living and producing new materialities and new idealities. In *The German Ideology,* Marx and Engels were not suggesting anything different: "Men can be distinguished from animals by consciousness, by religion or anything else you like. They themselves begin to distinguish themselves from animals as soon as they begin to produce their means of subsistence, a step which is conditioned by their physical organization. By producing their means of subsistence men are indirectly producing their material life."[58] In addition to the loss of the estrus cycle and the discovery of fire, what therefore characterized the emergence of the human species is this capacity to transform society that expressed itself, to take up the examples Godelier cites somewhat jokingly, on the night of August 4, 1789, or through the conversion of individuals and entire populations to Christianity in the first centuries of our era.

The paleontologist Stephen Jay Gould underlines in turn that human societies transform themselves according to a process of cultural evolution that functions in the Lamarckian sense of a transmission of what is acquired, and even by revolution, and not thanks to the effect of biological modifications. In humankind, in effect, exogenous heredity and the transmission of information through nongenetic paths made possible by language and carried out through the epigenetic process bear as much if not more importance than what is programmed by DNA. We therefore benefit from the advantage, unique among the living, of also being part of Lamarckian evolution, of the massive transmission of the acquired, which possesses a relative autonomy. This is why the appearance of the prescriptive, the injunctive, and the preliminary appearance of meaning cannot be explained as a simple derivation.

To realize the extent of this human deviation, one must make one's way through a series of subtle and reflexive mediations, through careful analyses and, in the end, through a veritable shift in terrain: ethnography, which is not reducible to ethology; sociology, which is not reducible to biology; and a psychology that does not limit itself to the neurosciences. Not, if it needs to be restated, because there is some kind of transcendence or foundation outside of man or within him in the form of innate ideas (what has been called "natural law") or any unconditional and a priori imperatives (what Kant called "moral law"), not because there is any kind of free will. No! What invalidates these various naturalist reductionisms and this confusion of functions and structures, this "vulgar materialism"— the expression is Marx's and it designates the lack of historical and dialectical thought in the French materialists of the eighteenth century—is their incapacity to account for the epigenetic enigma. Just as there are unpredictable and innovative events in phylogenesis and the becoming of living forms, there are, in ontogenesis and in the history of each individual, events, encounters, and decisions that are or are not preceded by judgments. In order to understand this strange spontaneity of the selected and the transmitted, the inventions of norms, this nonteleological succession of emergent properties, to comprehend the quasi a-prioris or schemas that suddenly yet variously and durably arise in natural history, one has to use qualitatively appropriate means. In a word, the time has not yet come where one will be able to articulate sensibly the three histories that Changeux says take shape at the level of the every individual's brain: the evolution of the species; the social and cultural history of the community to which the subject belongs; and personal history.[59]

Naturalists and geneticists have discovered neoteny, or the capacity certain organisms have to prolong their development. Man, in particular, seems to be different from the chimpanzee thanks to the slowing of his development and his prolonged immaturity, as if he, once he reached adulthood, had held onto the morphological juvenile characteristics of his immediate ancestors. In other words, one can say that every newborn is born prematurely, with ontogenesis continuing for the first quarter of a human life. Ernst Haeckel, one of Darwin's disciples, prepared the terrain for the emergence of the hypothesis of neoteny, because at the beginning of the century, he saw in the ontogeny of embryonic development the recapitulation of the phylogeny of the evolution of species.[60]

Yet this situation that depends on the observation of heterocronies, of different rhythms in evolution, was not devoid of ambivalence in axiological terms because in the 1920s, it was proposed by a certain Louis Bolk, one of Haeckel's disciples, and was used to support a hierarchical and therefore racist approach to races. Gould recounts one of the most important errors of these theses of hominization, which rely on ontogenesis and phylogenesis. Briefly stated, if European ancestors, at the top of the scale of beings, are unfortunate enough to have a child with Down's syndrome, this is because the child had not attained the ultimate stage of his development over the course of his ontogenesis. We know today that the malformation called trisomy 21 is due to a chromosomal anomaly. In French, the most common term used to name this state is unfortunately "mongolism." Why is this? Because on the hierarchy of hominization, the rank that precedes "Caucasian" is actually "Mongolian," itself above "Negroid."[61] In the terrifying racial context of the Second World War and following the advent of the synthetic theory of evolution, it is easy to understand that research on the role of ontogenesis ceased for a generation.

Now that elementary precautions against the "mismeasure of man" have been taken, how could we misrecognize this characteristic of determined genetic plasticity, cellular malleability, this principle of indetermination, capable of accounting for the human event and also of explaining both the appearance of *Homo sapiens* and what is at stake with the birth of each child? Perhaps Hannah Arendt translated this very factual reality when, referring to Saint Augustine, she presented the birth of a child as something that is unique every time. "Beginning," she writes, "before it becomes a historical event, is the supreme capacity of man; politically, it is identical with man's freedom. *Initium ut esset homo creatus est*—'that a beginning be made man was created' said Augustine. This beginning is guaranteed by each new birth; it is indeed every man."[62] To say this was to take the exact opposite position of Descartes, who deplored the misfortune, or the deficit of rationality, that inheres in the fact of having been a child.[63] Yet this overwhelming hypothesis of the irruption represented by the engendering of man by the hominoids, even of prematurely pubescent chimpanzees, cannot force us to forget the long history of evolution and the fact, so destabilizing for the metaphysics of what is proper to man, that we share 99 percent of our genes with chimpanzees.

No one has provided a more profound echo of this hardly natural natural characteristic than Giorgio Agamben in his *Idea of Prose*. He begins by evoking the existence of the axolotl, a fetal-looking bacterium that was long considered a species unto itself since it was capable of reproducing. Then, after injections of a thyroid hormone were applied and it lost its gills and developed pulmonary respiration, thus imposing upon it the habitual metamorphosis of amphibians, it was observed that it changed into a salamander. The axolotl thus appears to be a case of evolutionary regression, of a bacterium that continues and transmits its larval life instead of advancing toward earthly life. According to many geneticists, this seems to be the model that allows us to retrace the evolution of humankind: according to them, this happened starting with young primates who had prematurely acquired the ability to reproduce. This is the source for the occipital hole, the butterfly shape of the ear, hairless skin, the structure of hands and feet—each of these are characteristics of the anthropoid fetus. What is transitory for primates becomes definitive for man, a kind of eternal child. Agamben writes:

> Let us try to imagine an infant that, unlike the axolotl, does not merely keep to its larval environment and retain its own immature form, but is, as it were, so completely abandoned to its own state of infancy, and so little specialized and so totipotent that it rejects any specific destiny and any determined environment in order to hold onto its immaturity and helplessness. Animals are not concerned with possibilities of their soma that are not inscribed in their germen; contrary to what might be thought, they pay no attention whatsoever to that which is mortal (the soma is, in each individual, that which in any case is doomed to die), and they develop only the infinitely repeatable possibilities fixed in the genetic code. They attend only to the Law—only to what is written.
>
> The neotenic infant, on the other hand, would find himself in the condition of being able to pay attention precisely to what has not been written, to somatic possibilities that are arbitrary and uncodified; in his infantile totipotency, he would be ecstatically overwhelmed, cast out of himself, not like other living beings into a specific adventure or environment, but for the first time into a *world* . . .
>
> But this openness, this stunned post in being, is not an event that concerns him in some way. It is not in fact even an event, something that can be endosomatically recorded and acquired in genetic memory; it is, rather, something that must remain absolutely external, nothing that concerns him, and that, as such, can only be entrusted to oblivion, which is to say, to an exosomatic memory and to a tradition. For him it is a question of remembering precisely

nothing: nothing that happened to him or manifested itself, but which also, as nothing, anticipates every presence and every memory. This is why before handing down any knowledge or tradition, man necessarily has to hand down the very thoughtlessness, the very indeterminate openness only in which something like a concrete historical tradition has become possible. Which can also be expressed by the apparently trivial constatation that before transmitting something himself, man must first of all transmit language. (This is why a grown man cannot learn to speak; children, not adults, entered language for the first time, and despite forty millennia of the species *homo sapiens,* precisely the most human of his characteristics—the acquisition of language—has remained firmly linked to an infantile condition and to an exteriority: whoever believes in a specific destiny cannot truly speak.)[64]

If I have cited this passage at such length, it is because I find it admirable in the way it philosophically orchestrates the double logic of the innate and the acquired. In addition, the connection between the persistence of childhood and the possibility of language allows us to go beyond the opposition between determinist reductionism and metaphysical humanism, and in particular to put an end to the activism of reason and liberty that misunderstands the basic precariousness of the human being. Of course, many philosophies could be reinterpreted in the light of this unknown though obscurely felt neoteny: from Rousseauist perfectibility to Fichtean freedom all the way to that "shrine of nothing" with which Heidegger designates *Dasein*. There is therefore a substantial risk of using this hypothesis to further yet another false path through the exploitation of a certain existential pathos without restraint, the one intoned ad nauseum if not in unison by a certain number of philosophers and psychoanalysts: incompletion, lack, negativity, radical contingency, basic insecurity, human incondition. Only a new historical materialism attentive to the scientific challenges of the various naturalisms, one that would also recognize Marxist discourse's blindness to the inhumanity of dark times, will be capable of providing us with the conditions for both a sobering up and a democracy.

3

Between Possessions and Persons

Thus all natural history I had begun to regard as a branch of the political. Every living species came each in its humble right, striking at the gate and demanding admittance to the bosom of Democracy.

—JULES MICHELET, *The Bird*

Lévi-Strauss invites us to criticize the notion of the rights of man, which he affirms are too strongly anchored in a philosophy of subjectivity. He says we should replace it with the principle of a system of the rights of man as a living being, a right of the human species among other species: this is "wild" and pessimist thinking. Its austere analysis makes it irredeemable for the movements of "deep ecology."[1] It would certainly be a misunderstanding and a caricature of this position from an ethnographer to use it to claim, for example, an extension of the rights of man to chimpanzees under the pretext that we now know just how close they are to us on the genetic and cognitive levels. When I first heard this claim, I was moved by it. Later on, though, I began to fear that, once it was revealed and given over to the broader public, this excess of regard for the great apes might inspire political mockery and ethical exasperation. Outrageousness loses more battles than can be won through patience and measure.

A theoretico-practical aporia overburdens controversies bearing on the animal and its condition. But does speaking of the animal condition not commit us to taking part in a fundamental debate, to pretending to ignore that the dogma of continental philosophy places the human condition, or, rather, the human *incondition,* in opposition to animal nature? In France, most professors of philosophy who teach the great metaphysical tradition, sometimes through its internal critique, retrace this boundary, which, from Pico della Mirandola to Marx, forces us to conceive of man as a history and a task—and not merely as a given entity.

Marxism is a part of this tradition, as this page from Engels can testify:

> When after thousands of years of struggle the differentiation of hand from foot, and erect gait, were finally established, man became distinct from the monkey and the basis was laid for the development of articulate speech and the mighty development of the brain that has since made the gulf between man and monkey an unbridgeable one. The specialization of the hand—this implies the *tool,* and the tool implies specific human activity, the transforming reaction of man on nature, production. Animals in the narrower sense also have tools, but only as limbs of their bodies: the ant, the bee, the beaver; animals also produce, but their productive effect on surrounding nature in relation to the latter amounts to nothing at all. Man alone has succeeded in impressing his stamp on nature, not only by shifting the plant and animal world from one place to another, but also by so altering the aspect and climate of his dwelling place, and even the plants and animals themselves, that the consequences of his activity can disappear only with the general extinction of the terrestrial globe. And he has accomplished this primarily and essentially by means of *the hand.*[2]

Beyond the opposition between philosophies of essence and philosophies of existence, between philosophies of spirit and philosophies of matter, can we not say that Engels firmly reiterates this humanism of the hand whose tradition has been upheld from Anaxagorus to Heidegger?[3] In any case, the qualitative leap that constitutes man has a corollary: animals, including quadrumanes, can never be concerned with struggles for emancipation, a non-right that is "scientifically" shown by Engels. There is no sustainable animal liberation.

Yet this comfortable philosophical invariant of what is proper to man should perhaps not be called into question too precipitously:

from within this strong framework, an opposition of principle between fact and law persists. It is difficult to say whether this opposition constitutes the belief in our universal Occidental *credo* or *cogito:* one does not found law in fact, nor the normative in the constative. Philosophers such as Hobbes, Spinoza, and Marx did indeed dare to do so, but they went against the majority tradition. One cannot take proper measure of their unavoidable transgressions without having previously admitted and transmitted the abc's of the disjunction between the prescriptive and the descriptive, that dividing line annulled, sometimes for the better and sometimes for the worse, by naïvely immanentist thinking. Naturalism—whose sophisms were picked apart by Marx himself, in his early works[4]—constitutes one of the specters of our democratic humanism.

More precisely, it is the scientific manner of judging that we must always first of all recuse when we consider what relationships science and ethics should have. It is in effect democratically risky to limit the refusal to establish a hierarchy among ethnic groups to a scientific rationale, for if some decisive genetic finding happened to bring us to rectify the observation, this would imply that once new research has corrected obsolete data, the antiracism that was previously supported by science would have to concede the point to racism.

This is why one must first of all interrogate the manner in which biological, ethological, and genetic models are applied to history and human societies: an ideology of science leads Konrad Lorenz, in *On Aggression,* for example, or the ethologist Edward O. Wilson and other sociobiologists, to claim to prescribe a morality and politics that purportedly conforms to the imperatives of genes. In the work of certain zoologists, ethologists, geneticists, and cognitivist psychologists, this reductionism seems constantly heavy with the insidious threat of a zoomorphic, biocratic detour—one that is therefore fascistic. In this respect, the critique of social Darwinism offered by Marx and Engels remains a very pertinent model, even if the previously cited passage from *The Dialectics of Nature* might seem to testify to a metaphysical humanism that is unaware of itself as such.

This kind of a prohibition obviously does not mean that we must renounce making legal decisions while techniques and, as a consequence, social customs evolve. Yet it is the transcendence offered by what a democratic majority tends to demand, in the name of the values with which it identifies, which, each and every time, can authorize the regulation of the immanence of behavior. Rights cannot be inferred on the basis of scientific facts: either they are consecrated and proclaimed by the state on the basis of a metaphysical, transcendental-immanent conception of natural law, or else they are to be invented, declared, and proclaimed, proceeding from the history of men. This is why I will begin by welcoming with circumspection the so-called evidence of irreversible progress to which, in her presentation of the program for extending the rights of man to chimpanzees, Paola Cavalieri attributes the status of legal precedent: "Since Darwin . . ." she writes, and also, "The new cladistics school . . ." or else "The most recent work in cognitive science," but also, "The vision of the former, past world . . . no longer has a role to play in our contemporary beliefs."[5] As if she were making law into a reflection of science.

Without believing that ideas rule the world, one can note that when the authors of Genesis produced a monogenist narrative, imposing the belief in a unique origin of all human races, when the Stoics in turn and in another way instituted *humankind,* when Saint Paul declared that in the "new alliance" there were no longer to be men nor women, Jews nor Gentiles, masters nor slaves, they were in no way acting on new discoveries. Inspired and provoked by events, they broke away and promulgated laws, inventing and reinventing universality. It is not because our modern rights of man are disillusioned and emancipated from all metahistorical, religious, or ontological legitimation that they should receive their confirmation or rebuttal from scientific discoveries. Only a certain vein of historicism—by which I mean a deep awareness and knowledge of epochal events in the modern and contemporary becoming of the West—can provide an acceptable justification for the rights of man, that sober article of faith for our times. And if one invokes yet again the sociobiological occurrence whereby the historical and the social are reduced to the natural or the scientific, a manipulation that is not too far removed from the subject that concerns us here, the extension of the rights of man to great apes, it becomes clear that science, which will always provide new pretexts for confusion, will not be able to correct the abuses of ethology. This can only be accomplished through political argumentation, laden with memory, nourished with history, philosophy, and social thought, and attentive to the complications of conflicts and the undialecticizable event.

This capital reservation being established (in other words that it is through a metaphor of liberty that we must in any case start), how could one not recognize that advances in genetics and the cognitive sciences on the one hand and the irrevocable nullity of metaphysically oriented validations on the other, contribute to instigating, for a growing number of researchers, a new way of thinking that owes more and more to the "imperative of responsibility" than to "the principle of hope."[6] Scientists, philosophers, and jurists demand unprecedented measures that are less promethean, more worried and concerned with prudence about the future and with consideration for those living beings that, over the course of history, will have been mere objects of appropriation.

Zoologists, paleoanthropologists, and ethologists are researchers. This does not mean that we have to accept without scrutiny the interpretation, which, on the ethical and political level, these men or women sometimes disingenuously propose of their results: their studies do not give them means adequate to the task of unbinding us from that indefinable attachment to something proper to man, which, since Genesis, Exodus, Aristotle's *Politics,* the first paragraph of the *Discourse on Method* and the Declaration of the Rights of Man has been considered equivalent to our use of *ratio.*[7] The fact remains that these discoverers of the origins of man and his kinships, these hunters of similitude do indeed contribute to the unseating of *Man,* and therefore also the unseating of metaphysical humanism. Contemplative investigators, patient genealogists, and discrete revolutionaries, they know both how difficult it is to make themselves accepted by the great apes and how easy it is to scandalize the "belated animals" that we are. Yet, at the same time, it is their

sometimes almost ethnological research that converging with research in genetics and in the cognitive sciences, leads to the barely
conceivable question: must we not extend the rights of man to
chimpanzees, gorillas, and orangutans?

Before any critical examination, an initial remark must touch on
the way things have been stated. From my point of view, it does not
benefit animals if, under the pretext of scientific objectivity, their
defenders systematically designate men as *human animals* and primates as *non-human great apes.* One may concede to Paola Cavalieri
the idea of an old scale of beings, in other words the affirmation of
nonqualitative anthropological difference, without following her into
the *Schadenfreude* of abasing some as a way of elevating others—and
especially using those men who are lacking in the self-proclaimed
qualities of the human species as foils. Paola Cavalieri and Peter
Singer point to certain human beings as limit cases and sarcastically
exclaim *"Ecce homo!"* thus catching "humanists" in the criminal act
of classificatory incoherence.[8] This way of proceeding is not efficient for the simple reason that its immodesty and its impudence
render it fundamentally indecent in relation to these fragile humans,
whatever they may be, to that different human who must always be,
in a manner that of course is to be constantly reinvented, the *first
one served.*

   Why is this? That's just the way it is and no argument is needed.
There is something of the categorical imperative in the indeter-
minable element in which we as human beings evolve: this is our
culture, our inheritance and our debt to our descendants. We have
to make our way all alone, without any guidebook to the rules of
the game, and even when confronted with certain handicaps, we do
not need to imagine the choice we would make were we to be confronted with such a terrifying alternative: either a man or an animal.
Yes, it is through the affects of respect and pity in which the experience of history has educated us, and not through an a priori rational-
universal faith, that we in the postmodern era find ourselves obligated to content ourselves with the indefectible and minimal belief
according to which each human being bears the singularity of its

unique being and is, equal to all others, a part of humanity.[9] Against the grain of this idea of a community of humankind, which establishes the legitimacy of the right to say "we men," Paola Cavalieri claims to follow Darwin and Freud in inflicting yet another narcissistic wound on pretentious and predatory humanity. Yet what she says has nothing of what characterizes the hard irreversibility of a scientific discovery: it is simply an affair of the classical process of strategies of rupture: provocation-repression.

The utilitarian theory that legitimates her outrageous claims is that of the Australian philosopher Peter Singer. In his various works, this philosopher has proposed arguments to justify a truly extremist hypothesis, especially when one compares it to the many other theories of animal rights.[10] He effectively states his opposition to philosophers such as Joël Fineberg and Tom Regan,[11] insofar as he thinks the attribution of rights to animals is practically insoluble. For him, the use of a vocabulary of rights is just a "convenient political shorthand."[12] Peter Singer's utilitarianism consists in determining the just or unjust character of actions based on the good or bad character of their effects: a perspective according to which the axiological must precede the deontological. It is what is good, namely the greatest pleasure, and what is good for the greatest number that decides what is just. Utilitarianism, according to Singer, is a form of egalitarianism, since moral reasoning appears as the evaluation of the entirety of decisions ideally taken by an impartial, well-intentioned observer who uses his imagination to put himself in the place of living beings susceptible of being affected by his actions. Singer goes on to say that this act of imagination must include an account of animal interests, since ethical demands of universality will only be honored on this condition.

Peter Singer is thus one of the radical theoreticians of "animal liberation," and if he refuses the legal problematic, he is also opposed to philosophers working in the continental tradition because they limit "equality of justice" to moral beings. All moral beings, and this is the main thrust of his demonstration or the object of his monstration, are not "moral persons," in the juridical sense he gives this term, because their mental fragility leaves them, as the case may be, lacking in the moral capacity sufficient for deserving the right to justice. No significant moral property exists of which it could be said that all human beings equally possess it. And this is why Peter Singer limits what is essential about the equality to which he lays claim to a consideration of interests. Since beings capable of suffering and pleasure are the only ones who can be said to have interests, it follows that all beings endowed with sensibility must receive a moral status. The "speciesist" is therefore demonstrated to be the one who does not take into account or takes insufficiently into account the interests of beings who are not a part of his species, the one who, in animal experimentation, for example, and in industrial breeding, treats animals as he would not treat certain men: flagrant inequality in the consideration of interests.

Peter Singer can then refute the argument according to which animals have to be excluded from moral consideration under the pretext that they are incapable of having their interests recognized, and he cites the case of humans struck with the same incapacity: newborns, the retarded, the demented, future generations—these humans are not excluded from the moral community. We must, he says, stop making human life into "something sacred," because the sole criterion for belonging to the *Homo sapiens* species does not hold up to critical examination. If we kill animals that display capacities that a human will never display or no longer displays, we are being discriminatory since we are treating similar cases differently and are acting as if the class of persons coincided with the class of human beings. According to Peter Singer, who brazenly takes his line of reasoning to its full consequences, the category of non-persons includes reptiles, fish, fetuses, and newborns, while the category of persons, capable of self-consciousness, preferences, desires, and projects, includes adult human beings, chimpanzees, dolphins, and other highly evolved mammals.

"So far as this argument is concerned nonhuman animals and infants and retarded humans are in the same category; and if we use this argument to justify experiments on nonhuman animals we have to ask ourselves whether we are also prepared to allow experiments on human infants and retarded adults; and if we make a distinction between animals and these humans, on what basis can we do it, other than a bare-faced—and morally indefensible—preference for members or our own species? . . . Adult chimpanzees, dogs, pigs, and members of many other species far surpass the brain-damaged infant in their ability to relate to others, act independently, be self-aware, and any other capacity that could reasonably be said to give value to life. With the most intensive care possible, some severely retarded infants can never achieve the intelligence level of a dog."[13] The only thing that distinguishes these children from nonhuman animals is the fact that, unlike chimpanzees, dogs, and pigs, they belong to the species *Homo sapiens.* "But to use this difference as the basis for granting a right to life to the infant and not to the other animals is, of course, pure speciesism," an illogicality that consists in trying "to make the boundary of the right to life run exactly parallel to the boundary of our own species."[14]

One will always be able to find "nonhuman animals" whose life, whichever criteria are used, will have more value than that of certain humans. In addition, "once we realize that the fact that a being is a member of our own species is not in and of itself enough to make it always wrong to kill that being, we may come to reconsider our policy of preserving human lives at all costs, even when there is no prospect of a meaningful life or of existence without terrible pain."[15] One can see here that Peter Singer is not afraid of the final consequences of his line of reasoning, and this is why it is important to take this theory of applied ethics literally, as it was written and prescribed in the last third of the twentieth century, and to produce as a representative sample the positive articulation it establishes between the imperative preservation of animal lives on the one hand, and active eugenics, "even euthanasia," on the other.

What is probably the most staggering text by Singer is included in *Practical Ethics.* With a terrifying luxury of precision, he asks: "Would experimenters be prepared to perform their experiments on orphaned humans with severe and irreversible brain damage if that were the only way to save thousands? (I say 'orphaned' in order to avoid the complication of the feelings of the human parents.)"[16] The argument here is that, if these experimenters and those who approve of them refuse this possibility but accept using nonhuman animals, they do so out of an immoral prohibition. Why not replace animals with "fetuses, prisoners, immigrants, researchers and their children?"[17] asked an antivivisectionist who situated himself in this same perspective. How many implacable experimenters who otherwise couldn't care less for the interest of animals will retain from this logico-ethical junk bag only the fact that they should be allowed to work on material that quibbling like this has made absolutely available to them! It is no doubt the case that these "philosophers" are using an argumentation whose aim is in some way pedagogical: they never invite their reader to take action. Even if it is only for the cause of demonstration, it is no less scandalous to play with the idea of an experimental use of nonnormal or anomic people.

One can therefore only regret the way Paola Cavalieri cites in turn these non-"paradigmatic" human beings, in other words, ones who are said to be lacking in characteristics judged typically human—the ones she describes as "mentally disabled, severely impaired, the senile." One might note in passing the precision and elegance of these nosological categories. These "philosophers" would never submit animals to such a crudely approximate nomenclature! I will certainly not deny that we are indeed nearing the core of the questions we should be asking ourselves, questions that are formulated by certain theoreticians of animal rights with the same insistence—but with much more delicacy. I am only underlining that their utilitarian manner of addressing this side of the question of rights offends humankind by using those whose destiny has placed them in proximity to its most vulnerable members. Paola Cavalieri indulges in turn the favored exercise of zoophilic utilitarianism, one that consists,[18] according to the rules of a casuistry at which Peter Singer excels with a lack of civility that will have been obvious, in making comparisons between certain men deprived of the characteristics commonly held to be human and certain animals lacking only articulate language. This is done with the goal of producing the evidence according to which these animals belong to the moral community for the same reasons that men who are not adequate to the norms of their species do.

For both Paola Cavalieri and Peter Singer, it therefore follows that nothing if not "allegiance,"[19] that is to say an amoral consideration restricted to one's own species, a narcissistic criterion lacking in all impartiality, justifies our reserving preferential treatment to these *subhumans,* that we accord them more consideration than to those animals that, from an intellectual, affective, and relational point of view, attain a level that is equal or superior to theirs: the word "subhuman" is my own, for in spite of Peter Singer's denials, such is the categorization that seems appropriate to me for the context of the proposed argumentation. It is therefore in the name of *ethical coherence* that Paola Cavalieri finds herself obligated to accord the rights of man to chimpanzees, gorillas, and orangutans, with whose performances we are now familiar and who we know possess capacities that, in our species, are held as being morally decisive. We should therefore cease confusing belonging to the human species and benefitting from what is proper to man. Faithful to Singer's analyses, in which he invites us to imagine that we might, in certain cases, prefer the survival of an animal to that of a handicapped child, Cavalieri demands that we accord at least to *nonhuman great apes* what we accord to *human monkeys* that only live but do not exist.

Here again, it is first and foremost the style and the method, the empiricist and logicist way of proceeding, the lack of consideration, and the misanthropy of these authors that is saddening, for such confidence in deduction, even in syllogisms, and in I know not what decision-making powers of casuistry, prevents the exercise of that art of persuasion without which those who love and defend animals will never be able to broaden support for their demands. As for me, I have not been afraid to consider the possibility that there may be something of a proximity between certain deficient humans and certain highly evolved animals,[20] but I knew that the exercise was risky, and I attempted to take it on with the wisdom of love as a way of inspiring an approach to human singularity that would be less subject to the criteria of competence. Taking into account a humanity harder to bear and, paradoxically and mysteriously, more human, it seemed necessary to me to assume responsibility for those who are said to be "poor in world,"[21] which is the opposite of what

Peter Singer and Paola Cavalieri do. Their criteria for distinguishing among living beings are limited to integrity and performance.

Is it because it has proved possible to speak with monkeys that it becomes legitimate to attribute the rights of man to them? This incontestable advance in communication probably only strengthens the unease and shame that many men, even scientists, feel when their eyes meet these captives delivered to their mercy. We should have given these great apes rights a long time ago; we didn't really need to wait until they were *endangered species.* Abject treatment of them certainly continues, whether by the poor (in poaching) or by the rich (in experimentation), and this means that our anti-humanist utilitarians derive their power less from the capacity for persuasive argumentation than from their stories. Singer notes: "In a well-known series of experiments that went on for more than fifteen years, H. F. Harlow of the Primate Research Center, Madison, Wisconsin, reared monkeys under conditions of maternal deprivation and total isolation. He found in this way that he could reduce the monkeys to a state in which, when placed among normal monkeys, they sat huddled in a corner in a condition of persistent depression and fear. Harlow also produced monkey mothers so neurotic that they smashed their infant's face into the floor and rubbed it back and forth."[22] I mention this example as a way of underlining that the desire to make these psychic and physical forms of torture stop at all costs excuses to a certain extent the outrageous proposals proffered by the partisans of *Deep Ecology* and the authors of the *Great Ape Project: Equality beyond Humanity.*

In Paola Cavalieri's text, what seems most serious is a note that condemns article 3 of the Nuremberg code. Ethico-political insensitivity and a dearth of historical culture seem to join forces in this note, where she says she is indignant that, at the time, the judges recommended that any therapeutic or experimental approach bearing on man be preceded by animal experimentation. The Nuremberg tribunal only appears to her as the moment and place where animal experimentation was officially legalized. And not at all as the trial and historical moment when magistrates, horrified by the cases they had to examine concerning the cruel, degrading, mutilating, and mortal research carried out on men, women, and children, solemnly declared to the whole world that human experimentation should never happen again.

I am far from thinking that Luc Ferry is right to compare National Socialist legislation in favor of animals, the *Tierschutzgesetz,* and the racial laws.[23] This kind of legislation has existed for quite a while in the laws of the *Länder,* and as a matter of fact in the legislation of other European countries as well.[24] Yet Cavalieri's text suggests that the radical defenders of animals could not care less about the major disasters that happened to men because of men. It is one thing to take offense at the clean consciousness with which "prerequisites" authorizing the most often useless sacrifice of far too large a number of animals is practiced, to demand in accordance that alternative forms of experimentation, such as the cultivation of cells, be practiced as often as is possible. It is quite another thing to denounce a legal disposition that, in the historical context from which Cavalieri isolates it, definitively condemned the criminal use of the caduceus by the swastika. To indulge in indignation as soon as it is a question of the treatment of beasts without even mentioning that at stake on the international legal center stage was the treatment of human beings as livestock is an attitude that empties the argument of any credibility because its author seems to be saying that animal experimentation is as criminal, *if not more criminal,* than the experiments the Nazis carried out on Jews and Gypsies: "Cases of manifest ignominy (where human beings, devalorized by legislators as socially inferior or physiologically lacking, are forcibly utilized as experimental material)."[25]

To take the Nuremberg tribunal as a target rather than, say, the posterity of Claude Bernard's *Introduction to the Study of Experimental Medicine* shows a lack of good judgment and an inability to respect the tacit, minimal moral contract without which a discussion about what we must or must not do remains almost meaningless.[26] Paola Cavalieri diverts the Nuremberg Code, with its noble definition of the reminder or the proclamation of the dignity of every human being, to her own ends. She begins by underlining, in an inappropriate way, the irresponsible way in which experiments on animals were codified as fully legal. She then draws the consequences of her indecent analysis as a way of allowing primates to benefit from the positive fallout of the radical realization of the inviolability of the person that took place in 1947. For her, the Nuremberg tribunal then becomes nothing more than the exemplary occurrence of the tie that fatally links the proper of man to the torture and murder of animals.

One must not however believe that "animal liberation" activists were unaware of the objections that could be made to their arguments. As a way of making fun of his adversaries, Peter Singer even found a name: the "slippery slope argument," the situation in which we would find ourselves if the demarcation between man and animal were abandoned. "Once we allow that an intellectually disabled human being has no higher moral status than an animal, the argument goes, we have begun our descent down a slope, the next level of which is denying rights to social misfits, and the bottom of which is a totalitarian government disposing of any groups it does not like by classifying them as subhuman."[27] He is wrong to scoff at the "slippery slope argument," because one will find no better way to show the dangers of his own hypothesis. In his defense, Singer contents himself with stating that his goal is not to abase men but to ennoble animals, and that he will not in fact allow himself to be discouraged by simple abstract projections, in other words, by the perspective that there may be regimes whose "leaders are ill-intentioned." Unfortunately, the scornful weariness with which he flatly mentions these democratic apprehensions, and the slapdash tone he takes when he responds to them, will convince no one that this line of argumentation is innocuous. To prove the movement, one need only walk alongside him and watch him slide. And to witness a truly amazing slip-up, one can content oneself with watching Paola Cavalieri's vertiginous plunge to the very depths of philanthropy when she quotes the decisions of the Nuremberg tribunal with hostility. Her frightful reference finds itself haunted, whether or not she likes it, by the presence–absence of deficient individuals and groups of human beings labeled as subhuman. The worst of it is that she does not even seem to notice and that she would no doubt reply that I am making the human beings who were victims of Nazism *sacred.*

Merely listening to this petty sabotage of human fraternity, how is it possible to combat those who take things from the other direction and cite the reality of crimes against humanity as a way of better undermining one of the legitimate struggles of our time, the institution of a rights of animals, those who morally and politically recuse all defenders of the beasts by declaring them enemies of the human species? Would it not be necessary to concede that these obstinate anthropomaniacs are right to question the quibbling style and asocial character of analyses like these? These same enemies cannot however ignore that after 1945, European Jewish writers and philosophers lent their voices to animals, evoking intermittently or systematically the solitude, silence, and suffering of those victims of man: Vassili Grossman, Isaac Bashevis Singer, Elias Canetti, Primo Levi, Romain Gary, and the philosophers Theodor Adorno and Max Horkheimer.[28] They were the first to dare to allow for the understanding that the fate of animals sometimes looked like the fate of Jews, unless it was actually the other way around. This analogy is no doubt up for discussion, yet it cannot be repudiated as blasphemy, for it comes from men who suffered in their flesh and their history and who knew what they were saying when they evoked human malice. It may be allowed an obstinately "continental" philosopher to hold these fragments of nondemonstrative thinking for much stronger "reasoning" than that of utilitarian casuistry.

The rights-of-man dogma to which Paola Cavalieri negatively refers constitutes both a major victory for our times and an insufficient doctrine, because it too often allows us to avoid making political judgments and also because it tends, more than ever before, to isolate animals into a no-law zone. Once one sees a metaphysical egoism—both virtuous and inveterate—in this exclusivist humanism, one can only agree to fully support any campaign whose goal is to protect great apes from the poaching that will ultimately exterminate their species, and to save them from the experimentation that tortures and violates what we have no choice but to call "individualities." It may then at first seem like a good idea to construct a rights of animals with priority given to those animals who are closest to us from the perspective of resemblance without allowing that aspect to be the ultimate criterion. The discovery of the 99 percent of our chromosome that we share with them as well as the identification of a common ancestor nonetheless seem to provide us if not with the reason, at least with the opportunity of putting into practice the intuition of travelers, naturalists, and thinkers who, from the sixteenth to the nineteenth centuries, kept wondering if these great apes were not men.[29] Yes, it is appropriate to attribute rights to them, in the same way that—and not because—rights are attributed to human beings incapable of enlightened consent, but rights that that are not awkwardly mimetic.

Because the project piloted by Singer and Cavalieri is anchored in a poor understanding of legal precedent, would it not be better to take things from the other direction and propose a specific and individual protection of the great apes and obtain a *moral* status that would not be a *caudal* appendix to the rights of men, but the solemn beginning of an international ethical codification in favor of vertebrates or, more narrowly, of mammals? For other animals, farm animals for example, and those that the law calls "livestock," what would become of them and of the eventual establishment of their protection once the extension of the rights of man was locked in, as it were, to the sole advantage of primates? It would seem more astute and more just to make the great apes the first among beasts rather than the last of men. I do not underestimate the aporias of gradualist legislation, of the new casuistry it would bring about, and of the impossible task of placing animals in a hierarchy whose construction would fall upon scientists. But these problems have already been debated among European authorities, and it seems that judicious decisions have begun to be taken in the face of the moral crisis represented by a juridical deficit that has been unacceptable for a cultivated majority that is not limited to the scientific community.

The nausea one may feel not so much while listening to Paola Cavalieri's hypothesis as when reading how her argument proceeds thus in no way encourages us to renew the position of metaphysical and legal humanism. To pose the question of the rights of animals seems to me in effect all the more necessary and urgent given the fact that such exorbitant proposals can be presented, yet again, only to the extent that within our Western institutions, there is too vast a juridical void in terms of animal protection.[30]

A Universal Declaration of Animal Rights does indeed exist.[31] It was proclaimed by UNESCO in 1979 as a way of better echoing the Declaration of the Rights of Man, and it inspired critiques from many philosophers and jurists.[32] It incontestably presents the weakness of proposing a personification and of lapsing into anthropomorphism. The reform recommended in its article 14, paragraph 2 more or less, though without provocation, tends to have animal rights defended as human rights are, something that can only be interpreted as a utilitarian provocation. And one must recognize that two phrases in the preamble are philosophically puzzling with their stipulation that "all living beings possess natural rights," which comes down to relying on the hypothetical and controversial idea of "natural rights," a notion solicited from pretty much all sides since others use it to restrict rights to the rights of men. Yet philosophers laying claim to natural rights have never, except for Ulpien, accepted that animals would be able to benefit from them.[33] A second sentence from the preamble to this declaration also appears extremely fragile: "Considering that the respect of humans for animals is inseparable from the respect of man for another man . . ." In the final analysis and with precaution, one can no doubt campaign for this opinion, but certainly not as precedent. It remains that this declaration is, in its inapplicable generality, a generous, no doubt exorbitant text, and it should only be understood as a limit idea. Engels criticized utopian socialism in the name of scientific socialism. Why should it not today be our task to criticize a *scientific animalism* in the name of a *utopian animalism?*

Yet to resist the utilitarian offensive, one must propose an alternative along with a certain number of thoughts inspired by the a priori—yes, a priori—rejection of the arguments proposed by Paola Cavalieri and Peter Singer. For them, the vocabulary of rights is merely a convenient way of presenting certain demands but is in no way adequate to speaking about the interests of animals. This implies that no preliminary analysis allows them to argue their claims philosophically and legally because the (utilitarian) content of their claims differs fundamentally from its (legislating) presentation, which itself seems merely improvised. They seem to have remained stuck in a jusnaturalist philosophy and to act, paradoxically, entirely within the metaphysics of the proper of man. It is in effect this naïvely renewed metaphysics that Paola Cavalieri says should be expanded in order to introduce a disposition that is structurally and historically foreign to it: the elevation of an animal species to human dignity. She acts as if a powerful movement of thought, starting with Schopenhauer and continuing with Nietzsche, had never existed, even though it was nourished by diverse currents that helped to empty out entities such as essence, nature, and human specificity. The considerable change brought about by great philosophers working within their tradition, changes in terrain defined as genealogy or deconstruction, make the sarcastic remarks against humanist ideology made from outside this tradition look ridiculous.

In effect, only a patient and prudent deconstruction of the theoretical humanism proper to the metaphysics that, beyond the opposition between materialism and idealism, underlie most philosophies can lead to a respect for animals in their lives and in their deaths without offending humankind.[34] It can especially help in understanding that we cannot define or determine anything that would be proper to the human without seriously failing certain men, that we can only sketch out a negative anthropology, as there have been negative theologies, or, even better, limit ourselves to a decisionist humanism. Exceptional situations in politics and in society, in determinant scientific discoveries, give "calendar dates their physiognomy,"[35] in Walter Benjamin's words. They also give rise to decisions that, if they are democratically made, produce ethical norms. "The tradition of the oppressed teaches us that the 'state of emergency' in which we live is not the exception but the rule. We must attain to a conception of history that accords with this insight."[36] It is with this democratic connotation of accounting for historical catastrophes that we must accept that the norm be born of the exception and that the "state of emergency" reveal or awaken the decision. The experience of the infinite made on the basis of limit cases, once the death of Man and the death of progress have been acknowledged, far from preventing us from committing ourselves ethically and politically to the defense of the most vulnerable among us, as individuals, peoples, or collectivities, becomes all the more acceptable once abstract universality and fantasies of foundations have been grieved.

We will therefore modestly accept the necessity of acknowledging that our good old humanism—from which we must make an exception for the Renaissance humanism that we were unable to inherit and to which of course we cannot return—did not give us only fantastic results and that one can certainly speak of a bad dialectics of *Aufklärung.*[37] It so happens that an "exceptional" consideration of the permanent state of emergency that men impose upon animals would provide precisely the opportunity for a reevaluation; it would allow us to get away from the anthropolatry, which, consisting in merely placing nonhuman living beings beyond any possibility of the right to rights, will not even have been capable of allowing human beings whose humanity was or remains problematic to benefit from these rights without contest, even though they are particularly in need of our proclaiming, declining, and defending the rights of man in their name.

Yet we must go further in the critique of Singer and Cavalieri's presuppositions. The idea of human rights has a history that makes it improper to use as a univocal category. The American rights of 1776 are not the French ones of 1789, 1791, or 1793, nor those of 1848, which bear the marks of considerable shifts, to the point that they are almost in contradiction with those of 1789. As for the 1948 Universal Declaration—whose ties to the judgments of the Nuremberg tribunal are obvious—it marks both a recapitulation and further progress and is the basis for the claims of humanitarian movements. Paola Cavalieri herself relies on it, even though she affirms that these rights of man quite simply derive from doctrines of natural law and jusnaturalist philosophies.

Yet if one limits oneself to an uncritical recognition of this filiation, one will never be able to give rights to any other living being besides man, as the history of the notion of natural law proves: the Epicureans and Stoics in particular refused to accord the rights that obligate men to animals.[38] Their thinking was that if man participates in the natural right of all living things, he also benefits from a natural right of man as a man, a right proper to a rational autonomous agent capable of entering into a contract. If one does not deconstruct this tradition, a task that Paola Cavalieri, to say the least, does not take on, it seems all but impossible to venture the simple hypothesis of a possible extension of the rights of man to the great apes. If this is in effect the continuity between the jusnaturalist tradition and the idea of the rights of men, there is no hope concerning beasts. The utilitarian must therefore choose: either he argues and makes a claim according to his own notions and values, according to the logic of interest, or he takes on other mediations that have to be examined in their historical density and ambiguity.

We must in effect return to the profoundly equivocal basis that continues to trouble the affirmation of the rights of man. What are we really talking about? The rights-liberties claimed by the 1789 revolutionaries? Or, braving contradiction, must we add to them the rights-titles or rights-obligations expressed in the 1848 Declaration, which can be defined as the power individuals have to oblige society to ensure for them assistance, health, or work, for example? The position taken in this legal, political, and social debate will inform the pertinence of any reflection on the justice due to beasts. For without a deep—philosophical, historical, and juridical—understanding of discussions about human rights, claims for animal rights will only be muddled. Attention to the complementarity between rights-freedoms and rights-obligations, one that was wrought by struggle, is the only thing that will allow us to render claims to be made in favor of beasts more precise. The procedure that we can now initiate, and which consists in substituting the possibility of other proposals to Cavalieri's demand, is doubly justified: on the one hand, by the fact that utilitarianism imprudently borrows the language of law; and, on the other, by the certainty that a new thinking of law can be proposed as an alternative to utilitarian doctrine.

To pay tribute nonetheless to the utilitarians, one can acknowledge the importance of two major aspects of their argumentation, ones that do not need a doctrinal context to become operative: the idea of interest and the idea of "moral patients." Yet even these notions should only be taken up after a final, philosophical clarification. For Husserl and Merleau-Ponty, the only authors in the Western tradition who account for animals ontologically, animals are not beings of nature, not so much because they are susceptible to suffering but because a case can be made to presume that they have *worlds,* worlds that can intersect with the world of men. I adopted this phenomenological hypothesis, which implies moving beyond the still very anthropocentric obsession with the great apes, as a way of attributing to mammals, and more broadly to vertebrates, something like a culture, and to think of their relations with men by interrogating *Einfühlung,* an eventual capacity for understanding that would allow us to have a certain—empathic and intropathic—access to their world. This problematic has nothing to do with the hypotheses of Deep Ecology nor, more generally, with those of environmentalism. It would, however, resonate with what we might call a *pathocentrism,* in other words with a centrality of undergoing or suffering shared by all living beings, one that can be found at work in Schopenhauer's writing. Without useless brutality toward metaphysical and legal humanisms, a pathocentrist perspective does in effect allow us to establish the fact that the moral community is constituted not only by "moral agents" capable of reciprocity, apt to enter into contracts with full knowledge of what this means, but also by "moral patients," which includes certain categories of human beings and animals. We can say that, on the one hand, the phenomenology based first in Husserl and then in Merleau-Ponty and, on the other hand, the Anglo-Saxon demand for an extension of the moral community might prove to be a fairly winning combination.

A legal treatment of these questions would in effect seem capable of constituting a credible alternative to utilitarianism and, consequentially, to the appeal made by Peter Singer and Paola Cavalieri.

I will not venture into the considerable body of English-language writing on the subject, which is remarkably well discussed by Jean-Yves Goffi.[39] Joel Feinberg's work seems in this respect to be the most well thought-out and responsible. This American philosopher of law refuses to confuse rights-freedoms with rights-obligations and makes a claim exclusively for this second kind of right in the case of animals, as in fact of all living beings who, lacking the capacity to be legal subjects, are nonetheless capable of what he calls a "conative life,"[40] made of impulses, unconscious instincts, aims, and goals that can be either encouraged or blocked.[41]

Leaving aside this approach, one that articulates concepts of philosophy and law with a rare depth, I will now briefly explore the aporia that has far too often undermined the debate about animal rights. An illustrious jurist, Jean Carbonnier, could affirm that "one of the essential characteristics . . . of our juridical civilization has consisted in pitilessly pushing animals outside of the law."[42] And for what reason other than the great sequencing of the summa division, that fundamental—and of course metaphysical—separation that forbids any proximity between the statuses of things or of possessions and the status of persons? Suzanne Antoine, a jurist, intends in fact to trouble these distinctions by noting an opposition between civil law and criminal law: the civil code establishes an insurmountable barrier between persons and animals (assimilated into the categories of movable or immovable goods), while the penal code, which has evolved considerably in Europe, more immediately translates the aspirations of the social body.[43] To limit myself to one example, a March 9, 2004, law goes so far as to criminalize sexual acts performed on a domesticated animal that has been tamed or held in captivity. Property law thus finds itself called into question. A major contradiction nonetheless persists: animals, viewed as living beings, are objects of exchange. Sentient yet appropriable, appropriable yet sentient: how can we get beyond this antinomy? The animal indeed appears to be the only being in the world unable to be treated as either a subject or an object.[44] As a way out of this impasse, Suzanne Antoine proposes a special categorization, that of a "protected possession," of "legitimately protected interest" in virtue of the intrinsic value of the living being: one could no longer simply call oneself the "owner" of an animal, and property law would be more rigorously regulated.

In an entirely different way, Jean-Pierre Marguénaud, a professor of law, has shown that in French law, animals are no longer things but full-fledged persons.[45] From the perspective of contemporary French law, he takes account of the distinction between subject to law and juridical personality, showing that personalization in law has nothing to do with anthropomorphization, and that it therefore in no way threatens the dignity of man. He considers that "attributing animals with the quality of being subject to law leads only to the establishment of a juridical technique adapted, at a given moment, to the protection, deemed necessary, of the interest of certain beasts."[46] The convenience of a "symbolic promotion" and of a "juridical technique" in no way leads to a trivialization of the rights of man, for, he says, the notion of "juridical personality," not to be confused with a "subject of law," does not tend to erase the boundary between humanity and animality. In addition, Jean-Pierre Marguénaud shows that animals, contrary to what Luc Ferry argued in *The New Ecological Order,* where the argument was limited to the Grammont law of July 2, 1850,[47] are no longer things according to French law, but juridical persons. This was the case once Edmond Michelet, Minister of Justice, encouraged the abrogation of the Grammont law and its replacement by a September 7, 1959, decree. The sole article of the Grammont law punished only those who publicly inflicted abuse on domesticated animals: what were punished were not offenses against sensibility but only scandalous acts.

This is why a new decree ended up replacing this law. It includes a clause that pursues the criminalization of abuse but abolishes the restrictive condition of "publicity." Once again, this shows that the animal is protected for itself, and that it has been given certain rights. In addition, one notes that the protection of the animal in its own interest has made considerable progress since then. Sanctions have successively been stipulated for the crimes of acts of cruelty against domesticated animals, with or without publicity, of voluntary abandonment and serious abuse, and the mandatory transfer of an abused beast to an organization for animal protection has been instituted. The animal is now protected for itself, including against its owner. Jean-Pierre Marguénaud can thus conclude that the animal "is no longer an appropriated thing. . . . Just as there is a logical incompatibility between the right to property and the limitation of the interest of the appropriated thing, . . . it is difficult to continue to maintain that the animal is subject to property law. The new Penal Code punishes voluntary animalicide with a fine. *Abusus,* the prerogative of the owner, is therefore limited in the interest of the beast itself. The animal is no longer a thing or a possession to the extent that the new Penal Code classifies acts of cruelty toward animals in a category distinct from crimes and misdemeanors: neither against persons, nor against possessions, nor against the State, the nation, public order, nor humanity." In fact, he continues, one is led to think that this novel category of crimes and misdemeanors, "navigating between possessions and persons," will not be able to hold for long, and that the "technical" hypothesis of the personification of animals will end up being established given that moral personhood and juridical personality are already attributed to "any group endowed with the possibility of the collective expression in defense of licit interests."[48] The two necessary conditions are fulfilled: distinct interest and the existence of organizations capable of seeing them applied. Just like the moral person, the animal is therefore a juridical person without nonetheless being a subject of law, and it is this juridical reality that had to be underlined in order to stop the debates from being ridiculous.[49]

There is an implicit lesson to be drawn from this analysis, and it can help friends of animals to understand that we will never be able to be completely rid of a minimal amount of anthropocentrism, unless we take ourselves for Leibniz's God, capable of all possible perspectives. This egoic, "speciesist" point of view, if one insists on using that term, must certainly be modified, yet it is the effect of our finitude before it is the mark of our power. It is also the condition of our responsibility toward living beings.

"Speak and I will baptize you!" the Cartesian Cardinal de Polignac exclaimed in the eighteenth century, addressing an orangutan in its cage in the king's garden.[50] Today, utilitarians, partisans of "animal liberation," affirm that the great apes communicate with us and among themselves, and that it is therefore necessary to obtain the rights of man for them. It would certainly seem that logocentrism has quite a few tricks left up its sleeve, as Leopold von Sacher-Masoch knew all too well when he wrote the ribald tale of Diderot who, after having claimed at the Academy of Sciences in Saint Petersburg that monkeys could speak, found himself, as a way of proving this discovery, forced to dress up like that animal. He is then presented in his cage to Catherine II. Ill treated, he cries out, "Stop it, I'm Diderot!" What response does he get? "Any old monkey can claim that!"

4

Rhetorics of Dehumanization

But because the stag . . . was given the sad gift of tears by the Supreme Ordainer of things, apparently it was so that he could use them. The stag symbolizes the just man, the laborer persecuted by the selfishness of great lords and given up to the exploitation of all the parasitical agents of the administration (running dogs).

—ALPHONSE TOUSSENEL, *Passional Zoology: Spirit of the Beasts of France*

Alphonse Toussenel, a nineteenth-century author from Angers, left to posterity two books that were each extremely popular: on the one hand, *The Jewish Kings of Our Era: A History of Financial Feudalism* and on the other, *The Spirit of Beasts,* which included *Passional Ornithology: The Birds of France,* and *Passional Zoology: Mammals of France* and appeared between 1853 and 1855.[1] It would seem that the xenophobic themes of the first work can be found in the second, in a certainly minor mode, but as if natural history invested them with a new legitimacy. Should one hastily leave this production to its obsolescence without further examination as a secondary work unworthy of being reedited, or else try to explain its context and its structure? I will be taking the second path because I am moved by a bifid emotion and stirred by two opposite movements: condemnation of an obsessive anti-Semitism and Anglophilia and admiration for the richness of what must be named both an ethology and an ecology *avant la lettre.* Yet I will be deliberately avoiding a third possible path that would lead to noting a purportedly necessary implication between racism and zoophilia as a way of better undermining any consideration accorded to animals under the pretext of an absolute duty to humanity. This path leads to an impasse of both heart and mind, and the logical, historical, and moral inanity of this hypothesis will seem clear to anyone who reads not only Descartes, Kant, and Fichte, but also Jules Renard, Colette, or Romain Gary. Under the pretext of a critique of "deep ecology," a current in whose vein no continental philosopher has in fact dreamed of inscribing his or her work, this humanist refrain has become very popular today, but far from making the argument more convincing, it has in fact done the opposite, making its basic falsehoods clear.

One can nevertheless not start thinking about *Passional Zoology* without taking a few detours. The animalization of men or the animalization of certain men does not start with Toussenel, nor even with the nineteenth century: at the scientific, literary, and artistic levels, one can trace its beginnings back to the Renaissance. As a way of describing several instances of how it worked, I will look briefly and successively at the physiognomic line that goes from Porta to Lavater by way of Le Brun, the anthropological work of Buffon, and Michelet's description of several major historical figures. Without it being possible to definitively exclude the possibility of being in denial, this detour will not bypass or dissolve a question that has the courage to be crass when it asks how zoophilia was articulated with anti-Semitism in certain specific instances, but it should serve as a way of immediately refusing an answer whose cheap humanism renders it smugly brutal and politically counterproductive.

Physiognomy, which claims to decipher a being on the basis of his appearance thanks to morphological signs and establishes a typology in order to do so, dates back to antiquity and to Aristotle's apocryphal work, *Physionomica.* But it is one thing to describe this fascinating though hardly trustworthy way of reading the soul on the body, as Montaigne does, for example, and quite another to represent it, to attest to it by showing it. This will be the case starting in the sixteenth century with da Vinci and Dürer, at a moment when sight is placed at the center of all kinds of speculation. Already in 1588 in his *De humana physiognomia,* a richly illustrated book that was translated throughout Europe, Giambattista della Porta, a

Neapolitan scientist, had forged elements of significance borrowed from the animal realm, "lines of animality," and had drawn up a concordance between characteristics of men and characteristics of animals that allowed for the discovery of revealing analogies. The book provided models for artists, allowing them to accentuate the expressions on their faces. "By compiling ancient authors," writes Marie-Claude Payeur, "Porta creates precise didactic types that sometimes come close to caricature. He analyzes ancient busts and finds dominant signs in them. Plato has the high, sniffing nose of a dog and a wide forehead, indicators of naturalness and good sense. Socrates looks like a stag and has a stag's wit and wisdom while having been able to erase the lasciviousness inherent in that animal."[2] Porta appears to be an early avatar of the gestalt psychologists, since "a nose in the shape of a bird's beak changes meaning according to whether the bird is a crow, a pigeon, a rooster, or an eagle. Texts and images combine to lay claim to a veritable form of analogical knowledge based on a hermeneutics of the body."[3] "Ambitious" eagles, "libertine" hares, "cruel" crows, "distracted" squirrels, "envious" owls, "jealous" hedgehogs, "quarrelsome" dogs, "usurer" sharks, "crafty" rats, "perverse" chamois, "drunken" bulls, "vengeful" monkeys, "timid" stags, "voluptuous" billy goats: all kinds of animal faces drawn on the same plates as their human counterparts.[4]

The working methods of Charles Le Brun, Louis XIV's court painter, someone familiar with the pineal gland and a reader of both the Cartesian *Passions of the Soul* and Cureau de La Chambre's *Traité de la connaissance des animaux,* further this inheritance, but rely in addition on a physiognomic geometry strongly centered on the upper part of the head, with the forehead and eyes indicating nobility while the nose, mouth, and ears indicate servility. The angle formed by the direction of the eyes and the prominence of the forehead and the triangle that can be traced on the basis of that angle make it possible to "calculate" the character and intelligence of animals, the signs that mark their natural inclinations. This experimental speculation and the calculated measures of differences previously understood as qualitative allow for the systematic comparison between the features of man's face and the same features in animals. The subtlety of the drawing and the refinement of the calculations are such that Le Brun can, for example, paint a group of seven cows, each with a singular expression and therefore with a different character: meditative, vengeful, aggressive, curious, indifferent, naïve . . . And this is why Le Brun, coming back from the zoo at Versailles, could juxtapose portraits of animals with portraits of men. With the same stroke of his pen and with the same measure, the source of a troublesome resemblance, the animal found itself humanized and man bestialized.

Leafing through these images, one feels profoundly disturbed. It is similar to the moment when Mademoiselle de Lespinasse and Bordeu dream of the existence made possible by adequate genetic grafts of goats with feet that would free our houseservants and the blacks in our colonies from slavery,[5] or when Maupertuis indulges a particularly daring rant about the mixture of the species.[6] It is hard to know how to take this: joy at seeing the continuity between man and animal already exhibited; fear of the social and political consequences of this science, whether experimental or analogical; or memory of Nazi atrocities. I often contemplate the photograph of a Frisian horse that has the "human eyes" one can also see in a Gericault painting of a horse's head, a humanity already found in the work of Le Brun and Pisanello: sad, melancholic eyes that seem to look directly at you with their attention turned toward infinity. This photographer and these painters would not have said, as Heidegger and Levinas do, that the animal does not have a gaze or a face. Yet this should not lead us to decide that, thanks to the art of figuration, these artists attribute beasts with exactly what philosophers have denied to them. The painter who comments on Le Brun's drawings in a 1927 edition of *Human Physiognomy* makes a passing comment that might give us pause: "It is fairly easy to draw a human face that looks like the face of a lion . . . but it is much more difficult to draw a lion that does not look like a man." Would it not in fact be more worthwhile to be suspicious of these visual representations that draw on the occasionally overly consoling powers of analogy? If, before dismissing this suspicion, they should lead to the observation that certain human beings have perhaps less of a human face and gaze than others, shouldn't we then retrace our steps? One thing can reassure us: Claude Lévi-Strauss reproduced drawings by Camper and Grandville in the supplement to his *Structural Anthropology*.[7] It nonetheless remains the case that the nascent anthropology of the eighteenth century, the anthropology that will articulate *physical* characteristics with *moral* ones and will constitute itself as a science, can only inspire worry in its concern for a continuity that legitimates analogies between man and animal.

This is why Buffon's natural history of man can make us both uneasy and suspicious: does not the birth of anthropology coincide, as if by fatal necessity, with a preliminary version of racism?[8] Man and the body of man, "varieties within the human species" take place in the history of nature, in a continuity woven together in such a way that nature makes no leaps given that, as one can read at the end of the preface to the part of *Natural History* called "Of Man," the human is double and no natural history will ever be able to take the mind and soul that lives within him into account. And yet, the naturalization of the body, and not only the body of man in general but also the bodies of different races of men, even if it had already been initiated in a more audacious way by Linné, constitutes a decisive scientific advance and a relativizing operation of the human exception that entails the creation of a hierarchy of peoples. Whatever the case may be, the narcissistic wound Buffon inflicts on the creature of the sixth day was attenuated and softened by a dualism that can be attributed either to a noble's prudence or to sincere Cartesianism. Yet this "touch-up" nonetheless came accompanied by the ethnocentrism of the white race, heavy with the devaluation of non-European and non-Christian peoples: offenses imputable to a methodology Buffon calls "historical" but with all the characteristics of a tangled knot in which it is difficult to separate what is descriptive from what is axiological.[9] This is why we read that certain men seem "to have degenerated from the human species," and that they are "more vulgar than they are wild, lacking courage and self-respect, lacking modesty."[10] It is of course true that the morphology of the body and face and expressions are not the only subject of this abjectifying description. Behavior and customs inevitably confirm the diagnostic and prognostic established thanks to the observation of repulsive characteristics that Buffon would no doubt describe as hardly human were he not a monogenist. For skin color depends on climate, food, and customs, and "the varieties of the human species are but the result of variations."[11] It is worth keeping in mind that the author of *Natural History* is not inventing this all by himself: he limits himself to a fairly faithful rendering of the many sources at his disposal and is therefore not the only one responsible for these value judgments.

Yet how abruptly does he distinguish between the beautiful and the ugly, the civilized and the savage! And in spite of our efforts to recontextualize his work, the description of certain peoples wounds a reader who is a modest inheritor of ethnology and structural anthropology yet also a contemporary of racist totalitarianism! The pages on the Hottentots—"Run away, poor Hottentots!" Diderot and the Abbey Raynal write at this same time—leave one mute: the women's "apron," "the voice's articulation" that sounds like "sighs," the face's deformity, the "half-eunuch" men, all these characteristics naturalize the poor inhabitants of the Cape—to the point of animalizing them. The idea of degeneration, even though it postulates a unique origin for all men and uses the theory of climates, and even though its monogenism makes it fundamentally foreign to racism as we currently understand it, still claims to legitimately compare certain peoples to the animals with whom certain resemblances are found.

No doubt because he feared that the precautions of his anthropocentric, Cartesian, and dualist preface would prove unable to halt the rise of the continuity between man and animal and stave off the heterodox proximity between certain men and certain animals, Buffon ended up dethroning the ape from its primary place in the hierarchy of the animals. He remains completely foreign to the representation of man that Rousseau had called for and which was necessary to the constitution of a human science! "Suppose a Montesquieu, a Buffon, a Diderot, a Duclos, a d'Alembert, a Condillac, and other men of that stamp were to travel in order to instruct their countrymen, observing and describing as only they know how. . . . Suppose that, on their return from these memorable journeys, these new

Hercules then wrote at leisure the natural, moral, and political history of what they had seen, we ourselves would see a new world issue from their pen, and we would thereby learn to know our own." [12] Rousseau then indulges a remark that shows just how complex his thinking has become and the idea of justice that it harbors. "If such observers as these were to say of one animal—an anthropomorphic one that is sometimes called pongo, madrilla, enjocko, and at others orangutan—that it is a man and of a different animal that it is a beast, then I say we must believe them." [13]

Then came Lavater, who, though a fervent Rousseauist, was the author of many writings and several series of drawings that are all the more morally and politically equivocal given that their pious author pursued them with a philanthropic and theological goal: to lend visibility to the signs, either already visible here on earth or that will only become visible in the afterlife, of the eminent dignity proper to that human creature that he also teaches us to judge on the basis of his face or his profile. Without batting an eye, if we may put it that way, Lavater maintains that "the beauty and deformity of the countenance is in a just, and determinate, proportion to the moral beauty and deformity of the man. The morally best, the most beautiful. The morally worst, the most deformed." [14] This is a judgment that is completely opposite to Montaigne's meditation on physiognomy and goes much further than Buffon's descriptions of the calm certainty of a *kalos kagathos* evaluated according to his own image and resemblance. [15] Yet Lavater will not hesitate to cite Buffon's pages on the Laplanders, Eskimos, and Samoyeds, and will underline a passage that to his mind is decisive: "Not only do these people resemble each other in ugliness, size and the colour of their eyes and hair, but they have similar inclinations and manners, and are all equally gross, superstitious and stupid." [16] To which he adds, "Who will any longer doubt that a harmony exists between the inherited features and forms and the inherited moral propensities?" [17] With this method of descriptive axiology that authorizes a brazen extension of a *universal characteristic* to the biological and social level, we approach a so-called scientific study of "national physiognomy, as well as national character,"[18] in other words, a physiognomy of peoples. This elevation of prejudice to the status of science will be the source of Gall's phrenological theory of dispositions and the Lombrosian theory of the "born criminal."

Lichtenberg, himself the author of an *Über das physiognomik,* which Hegel cites in a chapter where he demonstrates the inanity of physiognomy,[19] recognized that "the earthly surface of greatest interest to us is the human face,"[20] but he cruelly mocked Lavater by publishing a *Physiognomy of Tails* in which he does not hesitate to write, "If physiognomy becomes what Lavater expects of it, we will hang children before they have carried out the crimes that make them deserve the gallows. Every year we will organize a new kind of confirmation, a physiognomic auto-da-fé."[21] We know that after having displayed a strong interest in physiognomic research, Goethe distanced himself from Lavater, and that Diderot, at first tempted no doubt by the monism underlying the enterprise, ended up refusing to participate in the translation of texts by the illustrious Swiss pastor,[22] and that Hegel was ferociously critical of him in the *Phenomenology of Spirit:* "Science if you like, immediate observation that is really only vulgar opinion,"[23] barely better than astrology and tarot reading, incapable at any rate of grasping the interiority of consciousness. Consciousness externalizes itself in effect *dialectically* and not immediately: in acts and in works, and not through the characteristics of the face.

It happens to be the case that Lavater was a patriotic, Christo-censtrist, antirationalist activist, and that one would not be wrong to see a barely avowed relation to this reactionary fight in *Physiognomy: For the Promotion of the Knowledge and Love of Mankind.* If we were to summarize the work with a poor translation of a fragment from Heraclites, we could say that for Lavater, "man's destiny is his character," and that this character can always be deciphered as a naturally and purportedly scientific law inscribed in the characteristics of the face, in the configuration of the profile, and in handwriting, all signs demanding to be believed, like the irrefutable telltale sign of a horoscope. The mathematic display of faces is put into the service of the occult as a lapsed project of differential calculus and aims for infallible divinations. This psycho-physiologico-hermeneutic theory abuses the otherwise fertile idea of *organization* and makes of it a sufficient condition for predestination that, as far as human liberty is concerned, is no better than the most pessimistic of religions. "Man is as free as the bird in the cage; he has a determinate space for action and sensation, beyond which he cannot pass . . . One of the unpardonable sins of Helvetius, against reason and experience, is that he has assigned to education the sole power of forming, or deforming, the mind. . . . Can it be denied that certain minds, certain frames, are by nature capable, or incapable, of certain sensations, talents, and actions?"[24] The choice does indeed seem clear: it is either Helvetius or Lavater, Kant or Lavater, Hegel or Lavater; it is either philosophy of whatever kind, or else the swindle that dresses irrational fatalism in scientific feathers.

In the final chapter of his work, which is also a compilation of all the authors that it seems possible to annex to the physiognomic enterprise, Lavater addresses the fundamental question of "lines of animality" and cites "the gradations of form in men and animals . . . delineating the transition from brutal deformity to ideal beauty, from satanical hideousness to divine exaltation."[25] This comes down to showing how one goes from the frog, "the swollen representative of disgusting bestiality,"[26] to Apollo and, in an analogous way, from the hardly human Samoyed to the beautiful faces of Kant and Newton. Lavater claims to have preceded Camper, the inventor of comparative anatomy who taught anatomical drawing to painters and sculptors, in his discovery of the heuristic function of the facial angle traced out between two lines, the first going from the hole of the ear to the upper jaw and the other going from the forehead to the same point; the measure of this angle was the naturalist's basis for the scale that goes from the ape to the god of beauty. In addition, Lavater proposes the measurement of a second facial angle whose sides start at the end of the nose and join up with the external angle of the eyes and the corner of the mouth. The narrower the angle, the more closely is the creature related to the animal.[27] "All creatures which we comprehend under the name of man, with all their anomalies, are included between sixty and seventy degrees of my angle of the countenance. . . . What is below seventy degrees gives the countenance of the negro of Angola and the Calmuc; and," notes Lavater, "by a further diminution soon loses all trace of resemblance to humanity."[28] He then asks that we look attentively at the three engravings that contain "proof," visible to the naked eye, of his *theory of evolution.* "The gradual transition from the head of a grog to the Apollo—which, when we compare the 1st and 24th figures alone, must appear almost impossible . . . exhibits itself, as I may say, in them."[29] We would have to cite all of the exalted commentary—the second to last paragraph in his book—with which Lavater accompanies the succession of less and less "ugly" faces and whose differences, whether of morphology or of expression, are infinitesimal to the naked eye.

But what is the status and what are the criteria at the basis of the animal ranking in this system? One chapter explicitly addresses this question. The physiognomist declares his adherence to Charles Bonnet's providentialist finalism and shows himself to be an adept of *Naturphilosophie.* For him, nature as created by God is one in all of its manifestations and at all levels. If an analogy is to be established between human and animal faces, this is because, in spite of man's incomparable—but not incommensurable—superiority, one can set up a scale that imperceptibly rises from the most humble animal to the most remarkable man in an *ascending progression of physiognomic expression.* It is thus the chain of beings that, by authorizing analogies, founds physiognomy: deciphering the meaningful expressions common to beasts and men is also encouraged by the most empirical observations of the naturalist and the hunter.

This *preparation* for a reading of Toussenel necessitates that something now be said of Michelet. The historian sometimes acted as an anthropologist, for example when he compares people from the Vendée to the Hurons because of the way they dance! "The fight, the ball, the mass and then the throat-cutting: everything worked of a piece."[30] At times, one would think we were reading Buffon describing the Hottentots. Following the great Enlightenment naturalist, these nineteenth-century authors in effect wondered whether certain peoples were not closer to animality, thus constituting an intermediary link in the chain of beings. These are questions that had already been posed during the Convention when it became necessary to discredit the "brigand" insurgents from the Vendée by any means necessary, even if that meant calling their appurtenance to humanity into question, as if it were not enough to describe them as savages or barbarians. In the same way, people spoke of the Royalists' "females." To the defense of the revolutionaries and their historian, one should note that physical anthropology was very much in fashion, to the point that Chateaubriand himself could compare a peasant from the Vendée that he glimpsed in London in an emigration salon to a ferocious beast: "He spoke no more than a lion; he scratched himself like a lion, gaped like a lion, threw himself on his side like a tired lion, and apparently to dream of blood and forests: his intelligence was like death's."[31]

Whether one had sympathy for the insurgents from the West or not, it would seem that at the time, in order to explain them or describe them, one always took recourse to the categories of natural history. And one must acknowledge that Michelet also plays at being a physiognomist, willfully animalizing revolutionary heroes: Robespierre is something of a cat while Marat looks like a toad.[32] And he treats the enemy camp in a similar manner: "I saw . . . the entire cast of Charette's head, molded on the dead man. I was struck dumb. One gets the sense of a separate race that has luckily been extinguished, as if there were several savage races. Looking at the back of the skull, it's the strong head of a cat. There is a ferocious bestiality that comes from the feline species. The forehead is wide and low. The mask is of a lively, villainous and military ugliness that would disturb any woman. The eye is rounded and deeply set back, the better to fill its gaze with fury and bawdiness. The nose is the boldest, most adventurous and chimerical that ever has been and ever will be. The whole thing is frightening, especially because of the unbelievable lightness it has all while remaining full of cunning, yet throwing life to the wind, both its own and that of others."[33] All of a sudden, Michelet turns into a disciple of Gall, and he goes so far as to read in this plaster cast a metonymy for the Vendée with all that fascinates him and repulses his republican convictions: bestiality, fury, a limited mindset, libertinage, Romanesque, nonchalance, peasant cunning, and prodigality.

In no way does it change the subject to mention now that Michelet read *The Jewish Kings of Our Era: The History of Financial Feudalism,* the book by Toussenel that was published with great and lasting success in the nineteenth century. He therefore knew both the book and its author well, even if it is very unlikely, as has sometimes been suggested, that Toussenel acted as a secretary for him. He mentions the book in *L'oiseau* and in his *Journal* on August 15, 1845, but without further commentary.[34] Poor Michelet is so often accused today of so many crimes, and in particular of chauvinistic nationalism and anti-Semitism, that a few words would not suffice to address the dark side of his great undertaking.[35] In any case, his works are much more hesitant and divided concerning past and present Jews than are Toussenel's intentionally polemical works. Like Toussenel's, Michelet's work also offers a dual entry into the historical study of men and the observation of animals. Yet so many connotations end up complicating any given interpretation, and the thinking and writing are of such a complex structure that there is good reason to limit ourselves to Toussenel's two works. We must also admit that they are more easily taken on and less intimidating, as well as being more likely to foster an experimental interpretation as we wonder about possible extrapolations.

Now for Toussenel. His era is, and will increasingly be, the era of workers' struggles, "The Time of the Cherries," and "hard times."[36] Philosophers, historians, naturalists, and utopists write in the context of an entirely new situation, turned upside down by the reversals of the relations between nature and culture brought about by the birth of industry and the reign of capital: the invention of the steam engine and the institution of the zoo animal; the discovery of the second principle of thermodynamics and the revelation of entropy; the birth of the proletariat and the development of social critique; the terrified premonition of the disappearance of certain species and the categorical imperative of a revolt against power and money. Does it really then come as a surprise if, for certain authors, the diversity of the animal world and the struggles of beasts with one another act as signifiers and even as revelators for social misery or, more precisely, allow for those responsible to be denounced, as if the only way to allow the people to understand the hidden mechanisms of its misery were to speak to it as if they were speaking to a child from the countryside exiled in the city, which is what this people in fact already was? In the nineteenth century, Hugo, Nietzsche, and Lautréamont all published bestiaries that name and organize the diversity of ontological forces. Yet in Toussenel's work, discourse on beasts does not participate in this genre because, in the guise of allegory and satire, it is used more specifically to *naturalize* the historical and social crisis by contrasting harmful beasts to innocent ones, by humanizing the customs of the ones and the others, and by animalizing social categories.

Yet what is truly disturbing about Toussenel's beasts is that they serve this function without depriving us of the wonder inspired by certain descriptions of their customs, or of being moved by the observation of the separation caused by urban exile and the announcement of the annihilation of the species, a catastrophe that had already begun because of certain human actions. In this perspective, animals do not then constitute a mere allegory. They play a tautegorical role in the sense Schelling gave this neologism,[37] in other words, even as they represent something other than themselves, society, they are nonetheless taken for themselves, in their own logic as living beings. "Let us not lose sight of the fact that everything is just as closely related and connected in the moral world as it is in the physical world, that series are engendered there in the same order, that phenomena are grouped together and placed at different levels with the same precision and the same symmetry, and that if not everyone is capable of producing the dawn of an era or the fall of an empire at any given moment in the same way we can predict the eclipse or the rise of a star, this is solely because the law of social movement is more complex than the law of sidereal movement, and that it is generally written in smaller letters in God's book . . ."[38]: this production of mutual symbolization is the way the system and method of passional analogy lends order to a reciprocal reading of the animal world and human history. In addition, unlike the German socialists, the French utopian has something of a vision of the apocalyptic supplement to human distress engendered by the new sources of riches; horrified, he discovers nature's fragility, its finitude, and the tragic resemblance of its destiny to the destiny of the poor. In a word, he discovers its "humanity."

At this critical moment of our analysis, a fragment of *Passional Zoology* needs to be cited as a way of giving a physical sense of just how far this poetic prose can seduce its reader thanks to the overdetermination produced by the double register of its writing, and how its seduction is made of dangerous terror and pity. In this passage, Toussenel is describing the relentless hunting and pursuit of the whale. Like Lacépède, a naturalist, and like Michelet, a historian, he predicts the future disappearance of cetaceans through extermination:

> And because I am alone in seeing all these things and in mentally attending this vast funeral, I who have not even the hope of delaying by a single day the explosion of the catastrophe through my predictions, it also befalls me, once again all alone, to bear the weight of my species' wrongs. My situation is that of a river hunter who sees his beloved spaniel leap into the water to bring a duck back to him, attempts vain efforts to get over the block of ice that blocks his return and witnesses all the details of the unfortunate beast's agony without being able to extend a hand to him. Whoever has not been a spectator right up to the end of an agonizing drama like this cannot know what suffering means and cannot have an idea of the atrocious torture I endure at the spectacle of my contemporaries' barbarity and lack of foresight. Happy are those who are poor in mind and also those that are poor in heart, far from feeling the need to sympathize with future misery and able to dizzy themselves with that of the present!"[39]

Evangelical, yet against the letter of the Gospels, this is a visionary and allegorical way of making the observation that everything has already been decided even though nothing of it is yet known. What Toussenel is staging here is an anticipatory fear, a tragic premonition in the face of human actions that "decreate"[40] the miraculously given, that exterminate, among other things, the whale, that strange marine mammal that nature was able to reiterate indefinitely.

For there are many other species at risk, and if they are to be saved, as Toussenel ceaselessly proclaims, there needs to be an entirely different politics, or an entirely different conception of the political.

> Assuredly, if there is a cause worthy of interest in this world, a cause capable of absorbing the ambition of a Statesman who truly deserves the title, it is the cause of these elite races threatened with future extinction. I am speaking of the elephant, the hippopotamus, the rhinoceros, the aurochs, the moose, the deer, the ibex, the stag, as well as the bustard, grouse and pheasant. Assuredly, if there is a law whose urgency is proven, it is the one whose effect would be to tear what is left of the final creation's most magnificent moulds from their imminent death. Yet it is in vain that the friend of the beast courageously raises his voice in favor of these noble victims, for that plaintive voice, like the white pelican mentioned in the Holy Writings, is extinguished in the desert and lost in the chaos of political discord. And yet each minute we let go by without undertaking this work is a crime of *lèse-humanité* of which the current generation will be guilty in regard to the generations to come.[41]

The accent here is surprisingly contemporary, close to Hans Jonas's: the same haunting evocation of a humanity yet to come to which it is as important to bequeath the natural diversity received by us as it is to bring liberation, happiness, and justice. Allowing a species to become extinct or contributing to its extermination constitutes a crime toward men: for this utopian socialist and analogist, it is mysteriously enough a question of the animal in the definition of the human, and humanity seems to be composed more of men yet to be born than of those who already are.

Yet, as has become clear, the ontological presupposition of his ethological and ecological project is accompanied by a comparison he calls "passional analogy" that he systematically establishes between certain peoples, trades, functions, or social categories and the customs of animals. Even as it provides a prophetic warning about our natural inheritance, this is therefore also an economic and social critique that proceeds through a selective naturalization of social relations. And it is precisely this postulated legitimacy of a classification founded on the correspondence between the animal world and the society of men and between certain animal species and certain social groups that must be called into question. The theoretician of passional analogy claims to establish series and classes among which men and animals are distributed in parallel. But by reinforcing the arbitrary good sense of prejudices, his operation consists merely in assimilating peoples to functions and functions to peoples.

The Spirit of the Beasts appeared in four volumes whose titles, as we mentioned, are *Passional Ornithology: Birds of France* and *Passional Zoology: Mammals of France*. These works were edited by La Librairie phalanstérienne, or the Phalansterian Bookshop. The cover of the second edition of *Passional Zoology* sheds light, whether innocently or cynically, on what we might call the socialist-naturalist stage by furnishing a clarification and two epigraphs. Under the author's name, it is stated that this is "the author of *Jews, Kings of the Era*" as a way of letting the reader know that this is not a simple homonymy. In a corner of the cover, two epigraphs are given in tiny letters: a quotation from Rousseau, who sings the praises of natural religion, and then a quip: "The best part of man is the dog," a famous line from an unknown immortal named Charlet. This is thus how the book aims to seize on kindness toward beasts pursued in good reformist faith by the Fourierist socialists that promote Toussenel! Not only does the phalanstarian publishing house guarantee that the book will display the very same perspicacity regarding the animal world as it does regarding society, but it announces that the anti-Semitism that has given the author his reputation will in no way be avoided under the false pretext that it is unrelated. What is more, *Passional Ornithology* and *Passional Zoology* further extend the anti-Semitic pamphlet. If there is a case in the history of ideas where kindness towards certain beasts found itself woven into an incredibly obsessional hatred of Jews and those to whom social hatred assimilates them (nouveaux riches, civil servants, usurers, bourgeois, English people, speculators), it is certainly Toussenel's. Schopenhauer of course preceded him on this path, but at least Schopenhauer did not forge a specialty out of the correlation between *Judaica* and *animalia!* The writing and thinking of the utopian socialist displays the faults of Proudhon's socialism that, because of a lack of materialism and historical perspicacity, mistook money for the natural-social absolute of an evil force it baptized "capital" instead of considering it as a historical class-relation. In a chapter of his book *Le Spleen contre l'oubli* that discusses passional ornithology, Dolf Oehler interprets Toussenel's work as testimony to the violent social resentment that was felt after the defeat and massacres of June 1848. He also emphasizes that "the vengeful imagination proper to Toussenel's zoologico-social thought is of a piece with his Manichaeism regarding the difference of the sexes and his radical feminism."[42] He also underscores Walter Benjamin's strange insensitivity to anti-Semitism when he refers to Toussenel in *The Arcades Project.* Referring to Edouard Drumont's praise for Toussenel, Benjamin notes only praise for the stylist and not the praise given to the anti-Semite.[43]

That being said, we now need once again to ask the question that opened this study: torn between laughter and repulsion, why not leave things at that? Because by doing this we would either be forgetting to add Toussenel's name to the repertoire of acceptable friends of the beasts, or we would be modestly minimizing, and in a historicist way, the extent of the complicity between anti-Semitism and zoophilia. It seemed preferable to me to confront this paradigmatic passional analogy directly and to avoid running the risk of a precipitated generalizing inference.

As a disciple of Fourier who inherited Fourier's ideas of harmony and attraction, Toussenel, it must be repeated, grounds the communication between heaven and earth and the correspondences between the three realms in something we could call an "astrophia." A physical principle of solidarity ties all beings of nature together, and passional analogy accounts for this with a method that alone leads to that true science of which naturalists and other members of the institute prove themselves incapable. The Geoffroy-Saint-Hilaires,

father and son, are the only ones to escape this oft-repeated definitive condemnation, "the unity of design of nature," an idea founded
in analogy, which is effectively in agreement with the Fourierist system. And it is the theory of passional analogy that explains why
Toussenel's pages on each animal species are strewn with references
to the actual and past states of society. It is this scientifico-occultist
concept that justifies the way he considers his subject, systematically
and naïvely focused on the French countryside, by proposing a classification of animals that shows no concern for seeking out an objective order.

Toussenel in effect establishes a first series constituted by animals "allied to man," among which he makes a distinction between
"auxiliary animals" such as the horse, dog, cat, cow, and ferret, and
"domestic animals" such as the pig, goat, ewe, and rabbit. For mammals that do not fit into this category, he distinguishes between
those that are hunted and those that are not, refusing to consider
those who are shot and not hunted, on the one hand, as being in
the same category as those who are run down and not shot, on the
other. This anthropocentric differentiation is reinforced through a
capital distinction bearing on the different ways of hunting. Only
the "chase" with dogs, falcons, or badgers deserves to belong to the
category of hunting, while "lying in wait" is actually murder: there
is the same difference between a hunter who runs down his prey
and an assassin who lies in wait for it as there is between the dog
and the cat.[44] It will have become clear that Toussenel prefers certain animals to others, which he does not hesitate to call "repulsive."
This leads him to make three observations.

First of all, Toussenel's repulsions are "legitimate" and "holy,"
because they emerge from methodological rigor: analogy rational-
izes instinctive hatreds. More than just declaring his right to his
own tastes and distastes, the author of passional classifications gives
them an epistemological status.[45] Secondly, his taxonomy is organized according to the relationship man has or thinks he has with a
given animal. Thirdly, as far as the beasts that are not allied with man
are concerned, hunting, and hunting as it is practiced in France,
constitutes the major criterion for classification.

For we need to return to the fact that Toussenel is a great hunter. He presents himself as having thirty years of experience, considers that his activity and his discourse on "French hunting" is authoritative. Hunting represents, he says, a natural right of man, and the French Revolution, were it only to have obtained that right, would have certainly been worthwhile. But in a paradox heavy with feudal fantasy, he also expresses nostalgia for that bygone era when only lords had the right to hunt and did so at great risk to themselves, respecting rules of honor, at a time when the falcon and the noble, both "chivalrous," were reciprocal metaphors. Nothing disgusts him more than the monetary feudalism that has now taken over hunting, unless it's the way in which the aristocratic horse has been led astray through racing and jockeys, whose name, he reminds us, is derived from "jocko," another way of designating the orangutan, the very animal that was referred to in one of Rousseau's footnotes. Money buys and therefore usurps the right to hunt, and over and against the "capitalists," Toussenel prefers the old Prince de Condé who used to be seen in his forest in Chantilly, standing still for long periods of time as he attempted to solve the riddle posed by the footprints of a deer that had escaped the hunters. It may seem surprising that this passion for hunting, and especially hunting with hounds, holds such importance in such a passionately zoophile and also socialist work, yet it is indeed to the accidents and nostalgia of this empirical activity that Toussenel owes his concrete and singular knowledge of beasts and his constant ability to find analogies between nature and society, drawing what he calls "apologues" from them. In spite of the little esteem he has for La Fontaine, these are all characteristics that make Toussenel a La Fontaine of merchant and industrial society.

For times have changed and the critical liberty of La Fontaine, a poet steeped in Epicurean hedonism and materialism who furthered Aesop's fables into the height of the French Ancien Régime, can no longer be exercised with the same seventeenth-century "honesty" during an era of reversals where it is a question of showing that the Jews, as the supposed incarnation of the radical injustice of money, have taken the place of feudal lords. Edouard Drumont does not miss out on the opportunity to faithfully cite his precursor and model: "There was no longer royalty in France because the Jews maintained them in slavery."[46] But what is a "Jew," or, to pose a question that means the same thing for Toussenel, what does "Jewish" mean? He writes in his preface: "Like the people, I use this scorned name of the Jew to refer to any trafficker in cash, any unproductive parasite living off of the substance and work of others. Jew, usurer, and trafficker are synonymous for me."[47] This definition will be more or less taken up by the *Dictionnaire de l'Académie* where one can read, in 1846, "Jew: we do not put this word here as the name of a nation, but because it is used figuratively in several of the language's phrases. One calls a man who lends as a usurer a Jew . . . it is said in a familiar style of all those who display great avidity and an ardor for earning it."[48]

One can discern in these "definitions" three polemical characteristics disguised as established facts. First of all, it is said that there is no need to confer to a word, even if it is a proper noun designating a people or a religion, any meaning other than the one given to it by a common sense that is then elevated to a people's opinion for the needs of the cause, the people's legitimacy to speak on the subject being grounded in the unjustifiable injustice inflicted upon it. Secondly, since the "people" treats the one getting rich at its expense as a "Jew," "Jew" comes to function as an adjective that qualifies any man or group who lives at its expense and any animal or species that harms its own kind. I do not know if Toussenel might not have found Jews who were not Jews (he did defend the actress Rachel against attacks from certain newspapers), yet, like Marx in *The Jewish Question,* he did incontestably denunciate non-Jews who are, in his perspective, Jews. Thirdly, the fact of being unproductive constitutes the major social defect, and Toussenel proves in this respect to be an orthodox Fourierist, since in one of his first works, his master had also imagined a city-state rid of all the nonproducers that disturb or merely do not facilitate the circulation of effective riches: women and children, military parasites, civil servants, the unemployed, sophists, and merchants. Fourier himself, who was in fact fairly zoophilic, also spices his utopian system and social critique with anti-Semitism.[49] Toussenel thus proceeds to show how Jews, who represent industrial, financial, and commercial feudalism, bleed France white by taking over the production and trade of sugar and railways to the point that France's politics has come to be identified with that of the merchants. And while he is doing this, he takes a dig at Saint-Simon, whose church counts among its faithful "quite a few circumcised men."[50]

In the end, through an endless oscillation between nature and society, *Passional Ornithology* and *Zoology* authorize the development of an analogy purportedly founded on certain human categories (the bourgeois, the informants, the Jews) and certain animal species, in addition to the elementary expression and brutal denunciation of the causes of social ills. "The marten is pitiless. It kills everything in the fowl-house if it can: thus the Jew, who has drawn the last dollar from his victim, will cast him on the straw of a jail."[51] These considerations appear in a chapter consecrated to "smelly beasts." There is also this: "The voracity of the hog is insatiable as the cupidity of the miser. He does not fear to wallow in the mire. He fattens on the filthiest substances. Everything goes into his belly. The same with the miser and Jew, who is not ashamed of wallowing in baseness and in usury to increase his treasure, and who finds no speculation infamous when there is profit to be made from it."[52] The same holds yet again for the minutely established parallel between the vulture and the character Toussenel spells as "Chaylock," which is worth its weight in flesh.[53] It would be impossible to cite all of the correspondences that rise up from the plume of the passional analogist as they accumulate thanks to an obsession that mistakes itself for a method. Unlike with Le Brun and Lavater, it is no longer a question of unearthing in human faces and their expressions the morphological lines of animality, but of tracing lines of behavior that seem obvious to an observer that hunting and familiarity with the countryside have purportedly made an expert. Given that this observer thinks of himself as at one and the same time the narrator of the "animals of France" and a theoretician of social critique, nothing can resist the work of this movement that oscillates between the humanization of animals and the animalization of humans.

As a way of concluding, I would like to interrogate the path I have taken. Can one say, as I have attempted to show, that there truly is a continuity in the trajectory that goes from Porta to Toussenel by way of Buffon and Lavater? A fairly long development from *Passional Ornithology* can act as an answer and a justification for this genealogy. Toussenel's Fourierism makes it impossible to decide whether it is geocentrism or heliocentrism that most strongly affects his anthropocentrism. Yet, like Buffon and Lavater, an indisputable inheritor of Galileo and Newton, Toussenel turns animal nature into a text that is destined to be read. "God, who created beasts only to make particular types of human characters from them, naturally bequeathed them with the task of writing this special monograph. And the sole task of the historian of humanity consists in . . . solving this enigma of feathers, fur and scales written in sacred language and then translating them into the vulgar language."[54] In spite of Toussenel's ambivalence regarding the fabulist, would it not have been preferable to situate the origin of this animalization of man and this humanization of beasts in La Fontaine's *Fables?* And more precisely, can Buffon's anthropological descriptions, even if Toussenel considers Buffon as just as profound an analogist as Fourier,[55] be thought of, on the model of physiognomy, as an *ethnognomy,* thus in some way laying the groundwork for the utopist's racist and xenophobic incriminations? Bouffon and Toussenel's works are certainly very different in terms of their register, their project, and their historical period. But we can see in both of these ways of proceeding the continuity of an effort and a temptation, ones that were also active in Grandville's work, whom Toussenel admits he would have been happy to have as an illustrator. The caricaturist is nonetheless radically different from the pamphleteer, for he is able to touch, entertain, and raise consciousness without stigmatizing peoples and functions and without denunciating purportedly guilty parties. It is also a question of a draftsman's talent, not the unwieldy scientific nature of a system that, in Toussenel's work, invents striking resemblances.

The credit attributed to empirical knowledge and techniques, whether observation and drawing for Porta and Le Brun, psychosociological observation and analysis for Lavater, travelers' accounts for Buffon, or hunting for Toussenel, seems to constitute a passional obstacle (even if for Toussenel, this obstacle is turned into a tool for research and divulgation) that blocks the possibility of constituting an objectivity dialectical enough to produce knowledge that can both protect nature and emancipate society. These different and similar enterprises inevitably fail for lack of the prerequisite philosophical reflection on the difference between man and animal. Fichte and Hegel are the only ones to have theorized the never tranquil and always mediated relationship that history sustains with nature through moments of self-consciousness. Yet even if I cannot concur with these philosophers without reservation, finding in the end that they renew a vein of the humanism of what is proper to man without confronting its aporia, I do note that in spite of their pejorative considerations of certain peoples, they do indeed give us a way to critique the naturalist–axiological deviation, which, with its mixed bag of tropes and values, is common to all of the authors I have mentioned, and which quickly leads to the tiresome iconography of the first psychiatric manuals, the demographic files of police headquarters, caricatures, and racist anthropometry.

The matrix of the obsessive aberration called "passional analogy" resides in a national and personal narcissism that can be expressed as an adage: Look at how I hunt and you will know who you are. For the demonization of Jews, of the English, and of speculators is supported by a comparison with beasts only because the inaugural gesture of passional zoology consists in dividing the animal world into two. In a very Buffonian way, Toussenel begins by declaring a preponderant interest for animals that, in the territory of France, either serve man or threaten him, and for those that he hunts. Then, unlike Michelet, who compares the people to the totality of the animal world, he continues by operating an affectively governed division that he elevates to the purportedly theoretical status of the passional, between attractive and repulsive beasts: martens and pigs up against cows and deer. He cannot or rather does not want to analyze whether it is beasts or men who are primal in this repulsion, for it is their immediately felt correlation that grounds the method. The anthropocentrism and anthropomorphism of the

French countryside bourgeoisie strongly arm the hunt's beater. Toussenel thus comes up short in the terms of a law of ecology that ancient thinkers and Linné had emphasized: the balance of nature makes the existence of predators necessary.[56] "Beasts to be destroyed" is the title of the chapter that concluded the 1884 edition of *Mammals of France:* the list went from the rat to the hedgehog and, in the same way, the world of birds found itself divided into the innocent species and the hateful ones: magpies, eagles, vultures, crows, jays, owls, and, more strangely, roosters and turkeys against larks, swallows, bullfinches, and robins.

The least that can be said of Toussenel is that his historical analysis is situated at an even lower level than the social Darwinism that Engels decisively criticized.[57] His work haunts me because it administers proof that a thinker, perhaps even more than a writer, cannot be both urban and rural without running the risk of making major mistakes, cannot be rooted in the land and participate in a movement of political thought, that, as in fact as already been observed,[58] it is difficult to be both a socialist in the woodlands and a hunting philanthropist. Toussenel's pamphleteering socialism will of course have the anti-Dreyfus and then fascist posterity with which we are familiar. As for his *Spirit of the Beasts,* there is no reason to republish it, in spite of its writing and the admirable pieces of knowledge it contains, because it is strewn with racist insults. This is how an oeuvre a man worked on all his life, under the illusions of totality and popularity, slid into oblivion until a professor of philosophy who works on animals and does not really like it when Jews are spoken of poorly found it in a used book stand and rendered it a saddened homage.

5

They Are Sleeping and
We Are Watching over Them

In man's case, however, perceptions are accompanied by the power
to reflect, which turns into actual reflection when there are the
means for it. But when a man is reduced to a state where it is as
though he were in a coma, and where he has almost no feeling, he
does lose reflection and awareness, and gives no thought to general
truths. Nevertheless, his faculties and dispositions, both innate and
acquired, and even the impressions which he receives in this state
of confusion, still continue: they are not obliterated though they
are forgotten. Some day their turn will come to contribute to some
noticeable result; for nothing in nature is useless, all confusion
must be resolved, even the animals, which have sunk into a
condition of stupidity, must return at last to perceptions of a
higher degree.

—WILLIAM GOTTFRIED LEIBNIZ,
New Essays on Human Understanding

For far too long, the animal question has been monopolized by the
sole question of knowing whether or not animals benefit from those
competencies related to the rational and reasonable norms men recognize as being within their capacity. At philosophical dramaturgy's
half-time, Descartes was the decisive agent for the excommunica-
tion of nonhuman living beings. In fact, for the majority of Greek
and Latin authors, and then for Christians, the problematic of the
logos was intimately tied to the problematic of justice. Animals,
aloga, those who were not attributed with *logos,* incapable of entering into a contract since they were lacking in reason and in articulate word, did not have a right to rights, nor in fact to redemption.

Was it not both profitable and legitimate to exclude them thus from the *logos?* It allowed them to be used and abused as tools, as personal property.

Belatedly in the trajectory of the philosophical notion of animal, philosophers will have nonetheless separated reason from law and the concept from justice: it is precisely because, they observe, animals do not benefit from rational thought that they are eminently worthy of respect. The originality of the meditation on the animal elaborated in a sustained way by the Frankfurt School can be explained in part by the paradoxical influence Schopenhauer's irrationalism exerted on Horkheimer and Adorno. Their thinking about beasts was developed as an integral part of a reflection on what reason had become once it was restrained and lost by giving itself over to what they called "the dialectics of *Aufklärung.*" Sometimes they date the beginning of this process of auto-destruction to Bacon, Descartes, and the Enlightenment thinkers, and at others to Genesis, when God gives man the power to name the animals, but also to the *Odyssey,* when Ulysses ascetically renounces the enchantment of the sensory world with the sole purpose of ensuring self-preservation.

For Adorno and Horkheimer, reason cannot therefore be reduced to the purely instrumental reason that manifests itself in *mētis,* the intelligence common to clever animals and technological men. If a critique of reason is possible, and if an escape from the skeptical circle is to be found,[1] it is thanks to what is for them true reason, reason that has the capacity for reflection, meditation, and knowledge for the sake of pleasure, reason that cares for objectivity and can become indifferent to subjective interest. The Frankfurt School's motif of the animal thereby has no real function, as is the case in the first argument on the suspension of judgment in Sextus Empiricus or in Montaigne's *Apology for Raymond Sebond.* This is in no way a *topos* destined to conjure zoological-anthropological difference and to ruin rational prerogative. From one end to the other of *The Dialectic of Enlightenment,* the animal is considered the most easily shown victim of instrumental rationality's domination, the violence of which is displayed at the abattoir, in the laboratory, and in cruel games. "Reason, mercilessly advancing, belongs to man. The animal, from which he draws his bloody conclusion, knows only irrational terror. . . . The want of reason has no words. Its possession, which dominates manifest history, is full of eloquence."[2] If for Adorno and Horkheimer, animals are pure *aloga,* the actions of human *logikoi* can be described as totalitarian since "unreasoning creatures" have always had to "encounter reason."

This new situation in the work of philosophers who never repudiated their rationalist option is so important that for them, the most pitiful thing about an animal, whether or not it is tortured by man, is precisely the fact of its "want of reason." An echo of Schopenhauer can be heard here. In *The World as Will and as Representation,* Schopenhauer wonders whether it is man or animal that can be said to suffer the most. Is it man who, by expanding his science, as it is written in Ecclesiastes, expands his pain? Or else is it the animal that is incapable of "the liberating influence of thought," since he "only gets the idea of death from death itself" and is merely a "mute personification of the present?"[3] Adorno and Horkheimer have no hesitation: the animal reveals itself to be the most miserable living being since, in its "world . . . devoid of concept," it does not have access to the comforts of "the organizing faculty of reason," it can only know silence, suffering, and solitude. "Even though the possibility of recognition is not lacking, identification is limited to what has been already vitally established. . . . Yet everything remains one and the same for the lack of any certain knowledge of the past and of any clear expectation of the future. An animal answers to its name and has no self; it is shut up in itself and yet at the same time utterly exposed. Every moment brings a new constraint beyond which no idea can reach. . . . The life of an animal, unrelieved by the liberating influence of thought, is dreary and harsh. . . . [They] cannot apply the brake of cognition to their destiny."[4]

According to the implacable logic of progress and progressivism, it goes without saying that "the being endowed with reason," considers "concern for the unreasoning animal [as] idle."[5] And "stupidity" can only then appear as a "scar that incites to violence."[6] The snail's inhibition as he holds in his antennae represents exactly what has happened to those human beings who are even more *alogoi,* even more deprived of *logos* than others and that are commonly found stupid (*bêtes*). Stupidity (*bêtise*) is always mind-numbing (*abêtissement*), because it is the violence inflicted by an exteriority on a proper body trying to get out of itself to explore the world, which thenceforth inhibits any initiative. Despite their classic reduction of anthropological difference, Adorno and Horkheimer can therefore make of the animal always already punished for its trust in exteriority the paradigm of human deficiency and, if we extrapolate, of mental handicap. The ultimate question left to us by these two philosophers, experts in "sad knowledge," is then the following: how can reason, correcting its works and remembering the crimes inherent in the dialectic of its *Aufklärung,* attribute a status to the sorrow and the pity for this "non-identical" entity to which beasts and stupidity (*bêtise*) are our exemplary witnesses?

Starting on the basis of the Frankfurt philosophers, yet also leaving them behind, for it was in no way their project to save the philosophical tradition, one can remember how, against an ordinary backdrop of destitution, the philosophical notion of the animal was an integral part of certain institutions and reinstitutions of reason. We can therefore meditate on three figures—Aristotle, Leibniz, and Husserl—who broke with the separatist vulgate, even if they never stopped to wonder about animal suffering. The philosophical tradition—must one call it metaphysical?—does not, in effect, display a seamless continuity undisturbed by a few (materialist, skeptical, and empiricist) snags. It seems that we should rather mark within this history the scansion of a discontinuity. For it may seem surprising that even as they identify the proper of man with the full use of reason, three great rationalist philosophers were able to resist the process of rational hegemony by refusing to dig out an unsurpassable ditch between the intelligence of men and that of certain animals.

Of all *delogations,* if I may be permitted this neologism with an ear to the paronymy between *logos* and lodge (a substantive that in its oldest use designated a shelter for a beast), the animal's is the most originary: older and more foundational than that of women, slaves, barbarians, and the insane. If, for all Greek philosophers, animals

are *empsucha,* beings with a soul, animate beings, for Aristotle and
the Stoics, they are nonetheless lacking in *logos* and in the capacities both ethico-political and theoretical implied by this *logos:* they
are *aloga empsucha,* animate beings, animals lacking in *logos.* Only
man is a *zōon logikon empsuchon* or a *zōon logon echon,* an animal
endowed with *logos.* One will note that Late Latin does not maintain a trace of this negation when it calls beasts *animalia bruta:* the
absence in them of *ratio* and of *verbum* has become so obvious that
privation of it does not even need to be mentioned. The passage
from *logos* to *ratio* therefore invites meditation in return on this singular, still somewhat wild and yet not Pre-Socratic place from which
the language of nascent metaphysics had undertaken to exclude
the beasts. The chiasm that appears between the works of natural
history and the more properly philosophical works of Aristotle in
the classification of living beings has been noted. In the biological
treatises, man constitutes a *genos* unto himself, a genus that is not
divided into species and placed on the same level as the quadrupeds.
In the treatises on logic and metaphysics, on the other hand, man
constitutes the classic example of a species, *eidos,* whose genus, *genos,*
is animal, *zōon,* so much so, in fact, that other species are associated
with him—the horse and the dog, for example. "Thanks to a return
of the repressed," writes Jacques Brunschwicg, "man regains his
privileged position at the very moment he returns to the ranks."[7]

The Aristotelian paradigm is in effect tempered by certain am-
biguities that it is difficult to declare as either merely allowing or
actively building solid bridges between rational-reasonable beings
and merely animate beings. In order to see this, however, one must
reread Aristotle against the tradition that the humanist-metaphysical
interpretation of his texts has imposed. It is certainly true that man
possesses *logos* while the animal only has *phone,* that the human being
is *logikon* and *politikon.* Yet, as Jean-Louis Labarrière has shown in
his development of the perspectives that Marcel Detienne and Jean-
Pierre Vernant offered in conclusion to their work on *mētis* (intelligence, craftiness) in Greek culture, things are far from being simple.[8]
First of all because there is an animal *phronēsis* (prudence) and even
an animal *sunēsis* (consciousness), which is not without relation to

that Homeric *mētis* that characterizes Ulysses as well as the cuttle-fish, the fox, and the squid. There are therefore certain animals that display prudence and practical wisdom. However, this *phronēsis,* in so far as it is diverse and relative to the interest of one species or another and susceptible to gradation, has nothing in common with theoretical *sophia,* which aims at a good that is the same for all, the sovereign good.

But one cannot content oneself with this distinction between *phronēsis* and *sophia.* For in order to define more precisely what ends up lacking in Aristotle when he deprives the animal of *logos,* one must first of all appeal to the distinction between two degrees of memory: simple *mnēmē* and *anamnesis,* the capacity for memory that is reserved to man. One must then, as Jean-Louis Labarrière does, return to *phantasia,* a concept whose function has been oblit-erated by a tradition that has, once and for all, translated this word as "imagination," in the same way that it identified *phantasma* with the "image," even though it signifies something much closer to "that which appears." *Phantasia* has been truncated in order to better place it in opposition with a *logos* that is itself identified with "rea-son." Yet *phantasia* is tied to practical thinking; it is an interpre-tive activity and not only a capacity for representation. It is *like* a goal-oriented form of reasoning.[9] It is "a kind of practical think-ing."[10] Aristotle distinguishes between two levels of *phantasia: ais-thētikē* (sensorial) and, above it, *logistikē* (reasoning) and *bouleutikē* (deliberative). It is only once this gradation has been clearly estab-lished that one can arrive at the question of what the animal is miss-ing. Benefiting only from *phantasia aisthētikē,* the persistence of an impression, which nonetheless already supposes time, the animal does not have the capacity to stop and develop the reasoning that pushes it to act in the direction of the future. It does not linger on the middle term of the syllogism and is not capable of recourse to a universal principle. Reduced to *phantasia aisthētikē,* which func-tions overly rapidly, it is deprived of *hupolepsis,* of judgment and opinion.

One can therefore paradoxically say that what it lacks is every-thing related to *doxa,* belief, persuasion, adhesion. One must then note that if it uses a certain *logos,* it will never be able to use *oratio,* speech. Instead of being immediately logical, linguistic, and political, the criterion for zoological-anthropological difference would much rather seem to be rhetorical, a register that designates *koinōnia,* the public and human space of deliberation. In fact, it is the ethico-rhetorical more than the rational that makes for the specificity of the human, and it is only once what *phantasia* consists in has been posed that one can understand the opposition between human *logos* and animal *phone.* The latter only produces *semeia,* signs and significations, while the *logos* is capable of *hupolepsis,* opinion and judgment, and produces *sumbola* and *onomata,* words composed in accordance with articulations and conventions. This is one way of understanding the definition: "Man is the more than perfect living being that emits phonemes."[11]

What makes the properly human problematic in Aristotle's work is the fact that the differences between animals, including man, are not so much differences of nature as of degree, and that this gradualism is superposed with the regime of *ōs,* of the "like," with the register of resemblance by analogy (a difference of nature) and even with the register of *osanōs,* of the "as if." Aristotle says that animals are "more or less" capable of *phronēsis.* But when *phronēsis* is said to be something *like* a reasoning and also something *like* practical thinking, when *phantasia* is described *as* a goal-oriented form of reasoning, "*like* a kind of thinking," when it is "*as if* animals calculated time and distance,"[12] one must wonder to what extent the scale of living beings and analogy validate one another and just what the ontological status of these epistemological *like*s and *as if*s is. We will not be able to answer this question here, but it is important that it be posed in order to emphasize the ambiguity of a distinction that was hastily established as a foundational opposition, and because we will also observe this nonrhetorical analogical operator function in the work of Leibniz and Husserl.

While for the Ancients the animal question stemmed from the problematic of the cosmos, starting with Descartes it tends to be linked to theories of knowledge. This is the case, for example, with

Hume in the chapter of the *Treatise of Human Nature* called "Of the Reason of Animals." Yet for Leibniz as for Aristotle, there is a parallelism between physics, psychology, logic, and ontology. And because the mechanism cannot take the living into account, it will prove necessary to return to Aristotle and "substantial forms," the active principle of "primitive entelechy," and to attribute "indefectible souls" to the "brutes." "The soul of beasts" represents a problem not of theology but of fact, one that has to be resolved experimentally, with a microscope. And the question of the soul leads to interrogating the right we attribute to ourselves, the tyranny that we exert over animals. The fact that Leibniz reestablished innatism against Locke, and therefore the human exceptionality of the relation to God, adds a troubling hesitation to the new thinking of the continuous. A hierarchical order being imposed on the diversity of beings by the hypothesis of the full, the principle of continuity would force an uninterrupted multiplication of intermediary creatures between men and God. Yet, as is the case with the Stoics, the scale of beings is interrupted.

If all monads are susceptible of activity,[13] the ones that constitute souls tied to the bodies of beasts are more or less unconscious, more or less passive. There exists, however, no more of a purely passive substance than there is perfect rest or a perfect absence of perception,[14] as the "new system of the nature" teaches it. The degrees the souls of beasts represent are noted against the inexhaustible backdrop of obscure, unclear, infinitesimal "little perceptions"[15]: blind thoughts common to all living beings. There is a multitude of murmuring solicitations that await only "a tiny occasion for memory to awaken, to go from being enveloped by the unclear to developing the distinct."[16] It is these *cogitate caeca,* these blind, imperceptible, and uninterrupted thoughts that ensure the faultless continuity between sensibility and understanding, between apparent inertia and the living.[17] The principle of continuity according to which there must not be a hiatus in concatenation is the grounds for the rigorous analogy among the monads' different degrees of perception, consciousness, and being. At the lowest degree on the scale, one finds the *mens momentanea,* a degraded spirit that dissipates into the moment because it lacks memory. Corresponding to it on the level of perception, one finds lethargy,[18] a state of sleep or evanescence that is not dead or inert, constituted in the ontological order by mineral matter. Above it, one finds the blind thoughts to which the realm of the vegetal corresponds and which is comparable to fainting. Above this, one finds perception accompanied by memory, that is to say feeling, still close to dizziness, to which corresponds the animal realm with, as Leibniz notes, all its degrees of perception of consciousness that can rise to apperception or reflexive consciousness. And finally the highest level, the apperception of the existence in and of itself of the universe, reflection, intention, reason, personal identity, the soul endowed not only with indefectibility but with immortality, fully awakened life.

Between man and animal, Leibniz does, however, install a border over which an understanding capable of rational sequences erupts rather than emerges, resulting in necessary and universal propositions, that is to say consecutions, and differing entirely from that of beasts. Human understanding is also capable of an excellence of memory, in so far as it ensures identity, responsibility, and freedom. The philosopher concedes a minimum to dualist discontinuism—"in nature everything happens by degrees, and nothing by jumps"[19]— and assents to the idea that the highest thoughts are prepared by, if not founded in, "little perceptions." For this to be the case, one has to accept that the law of continuity demands or tolerates a derogation: man, as reason and as person. This is a singularity whose revelation seems difficult to justify "naturally"—and not miraculously— if one thinks, on the one hand, of the heightened degree of memory, consecution, and even apperception of which certain animals show they are capable and, on the other hand, of the slight elevation above quasi-animality that characterizes men who content themselves with empirical consecutions. Not to mention the situation of torpor characteristic of those men Locke calls "imbeciles" and that Leibniz names the "innocent."

Anthropological difference therefore presents a problem for the philosopher, since, on the scale of beings, man both is and is not in continuity with the animal most gifted with perception and memory.

To save the system of the continuous, Leibniz considered three hypotheses. The first, rather Augustinian hypothesis is the "miraculous creation," each time, of a man, not a continued creation—in the style of Descartes, for whom God recreated the world at every instant—but a continuous creation inscribed in time. Because of the theory of the preexistent germs, the organism preexists, but, at the moment a human being is conceived, God miraculously annihilates the animal soul and replaces it with a reasonable soul. "Those souls which one day shall be human souls, like those of other species, have been in the seed, and in the progenitors as far back as Adam . . . always in a kind of organic body."[20] Yet the soul, which only existed at that point as a sensitive or animal soul gifted with perception and feeling yet lacking in reason, remained in that state until the moment of the generation of the man to whom it was destined, and it is only at that point that it would, according to Leibniz, have been endowed with reason.

Second hypothesis: the miraculous "transcreation" of the animal soul into a reasonable soul at the moment of conception,[21] which excludes the annihilation of the primitive soul. Souls can only be engendered by other souls and cannot be naturally born; as a consequence, sentient souls are preexistent in seeds and are elevated to reason "when the man to whom this soul should belong was conceived, and when the organic body, always accompanying this soul from the beginning, but under many changes, was determined for forming the human body."[22] Third hypothesis: because certain animalcules, which, since creation, reside in seeds, are destined to attain human nature, they envelop reason, which will one day appear in them. At this point, Leibniz replaces "transcreation" with "translation," which gains his favor because it explains naturally, and not miraculously, how the rational is born out of the simply animate. Certain bodies associated with certain souls would contain an aptitude for reason from the beginning, an aptitude destined to be actualized when its time comes. One therefore notes that the difficulty of reconciling the natural history of physics and a panpsychic and continuist metaphysics with Revelation is not easily surmounted, and that the status of the *animalia bruta* varies almost entirely according to which hypothesis one chooses. Only "translation" establishes a seamless transition between the sentient and the rational, between man and beast. Personally, I have always admired Leibniz for the virtuosic sinuosity of his confusion.

More than two centuries after Leibniz, "animality" finds itself at the heart of Husserlian thinking. One can realize the extent of this thematic only if one bears in mind the very movement of the phenomenological method.[23] A genealogy that is an archeology allows for the reconstruction of the original sphere of the noncategorical, preordained, preconstituted, prereflexive, preconceptual rational. One can decide to consider the different designations that allow Husserl to name this primordial layer as equivalent: *Erfahrung*, "passive constitution," "passive synthesis," *Lebenswelt*, "intentional life," "transcendental life," but also, more enigmatically, "transcendental logic" and *Animalien*. These are several versions of the anonymous, universal, and not exclusively human basis of a belief in the world that precedes and exceeds apperception, reflection, and judgments with universal validity. Between the original driven-perceptive-affective-temporalizing passivity and the belated reflexive-predicative activity, in other words between the different levels of transcendental subjectivity, there is a continuity and a never broken solidarity, even if this dark sphere is covered over by logical and scientific idealities formed on its basis and that relegate it to oblivion. Yet we must also understand how the dismemberment of idealities leaves a logical residue, that the pre-given world is already filled with evidence, judgments, operations of signification, that there is a logic to the pre-logical layers, and that the primordial layer is always already, through a teleological movement, taken up by the rational.

This approach represents a crucial moment in the history of rationality, for it amputates reason from its sovereignty, rehabilitates passivity by making it into a synthesis, reveals the relinquishment of the transcendental subject, inverses the logical tradition, widens the *logos,* and, finally, accounts for the first idealizations through which a subject is constituted as a *self* by anchoring it in a genetic egology.[24] It submits the rational to the subjective conditions of its constitution and frees itself to a certain extent from gnosiology, situating itself beyond the opposition between the theoretical and the practical. Above all, it links rationality to "animality." Husserl in effect names the constitutive sphere common to men and animals. But in this case, what does he say about the beasts themselves? Animals, or at least the more evolved animals, have to possess a soul, a psychic life, a practical and axiological ego, and they must not be beings of nature but subjects that have intentions to worlds, and perhaps even cooperate with us in the constitution of the world. "Their purely animal conscious life is focused, and the expression of a subject for consciousness encloses something analogous or else more general than the human ego. . . . This is something for which we possess no adequate term."[25] In addition, the recusal of a disjunction between being awake and being asleep allows Husserl to establish a troubling analogy between the more evolved animal and the insufficiently watchful man, making intermediary beings of all men who, whether abnormal or anomic, are more or less, and in different ways, asleep: infants, old people, primitives, the insane. Through the degrees of animality they represent, there is no link missing on the scale of intentionality correlative to worlds.

However, if preconstitution (animality) is always already in some way a transcendental logic, how can it be valid for beasts whose intentional life is not traversed by a rational aim, who are incapable of *epoché*, reduction, *cogito* and to whom the higher layer of theoretical thinking is in some way not destined? Even if it implies contradicting himself, Husserl will propose a description of the animal that is barely compatible with the construction of animality. He thus ends up listing the roster of clichés of traditional rationalism and idealism, sketching out a "privative zoology" actually far inferior to Heidegger's. Animals are incapable of reflexive conversion, are not capable of exercising "reduction" or of taking part in communities of "persons" oriented toward interminable tasks. Each animal generation is a repetition, with the set of types proper to its species. Animals do not have experiences, lacking as they are in a consciousness of the unity of their lives and of the unity of time. Not endowed with a consciousness of the succession of generations, they don't have a veritable common surrounding world. They possess neither "veritable memory," nor "intuitive imaginary representations," nor "anticipatory images representing the future," nor an "intuitively represented past."[26] They only have "obscure drives" that can "come into play with instinctual in-filling that do not however become representations."[27] They do not have access to the "sameness" of things except in the form of a primitive recognition that is not capable of returning to the past thanks to "memory."[28] This is why "their conscience does not reach knowledge of a world that includes things that subsist and persist in time." Finally, they do not have language, even if they understand one another and sonorous expressions. Here, one can see that the *logos* of metaphysical humanism comes back into play as a powerful instrument for the destitution of non-human living beings. Is it the phenomenological revaluation that authorizes this list of platitudes?

In spite of it all, Husserl seemed to propose the beginnings—or was it just a semblance?—of a solution to the contradiction between universal animality and the destinal deficiency of beasts. Here again, the solution resides in an *als ob,* an "as if," but it differs both from the Aristotelian "as" and from the Stoic "as if": it may have a relation to Kant's "as if," "that most elevated viewpoint of transcendental philosophy," which requires, in view of progress in theory and in practice, going *analogically* toward the noumenal realm even if, from a theoretical point of view, our concepts do not contain knowledge of objects capable of experience. In this case, it is *Einfühlung,* or empathy between living beings and between subjects that, proceeding analogously but never falling into the trap of the naïve facilities of anthropomorphism, authorizes us to lend to more highly evolved animals, in other words, to those who are not like quasi-plants in a state of torpor, mental operations similar to ours. This is a *restricted* anthropomorphism.

"At first, man, *a rational animal,* necessarily interprets 'blindly instinctive' intentionality . . . as a constituent element of the surrounding world: *as if* beasts were in fact some kind of inferior men, *as if* they also had being, complexes of being and goals directed toward being, toward the pre-given surrounding world, *as if* they had representations of what must be, *as if,* instead of their feelings, which are simple blind modes of instinctual life, they had human values . . ."[29] Because *Einfühlung* is an action proper to the transcendental attitude, Husserl can give a rigorous status to the "as if." To the extent that human psychology, that of the normal, awake, adult European, represents "preliminary psychology," which itself depends authentically on the experience and reciprocity of intentionalities, animal psychology can only be constructed, if not derivative. It is therefore good methodology to attribute to beasts that which we, as rational animals, possess as well. Analogy, intropathy, and the process of the "as if" have nothing arbitrary and naïve about them, inasmuch as the level of crude and instinctual intentionality that, with varying degrees of complexity dependent upon the species composes animal consciousness and its surrounding world, is not foreign to the original psychic layer of those who give the world to themselves and to one another. It is not an imaginary projection that creates resemblance; it is an analogy that motivates a transfer.

Yet Husserl will go even further when he wonders about domestic animals. Are "these not already really analogous to men? Do they not already really have a human though very inferior personality, only one that is incapable of continuing to develop beyond their beginnings as our children of men do?"[30] What does this remarkable "really" mean? Are we not yet again moving away from animality? Heidegger will offer scathing criticism of this kind of problematic. Husserl seems in effect to encounter a veritable aporia when it is a question of articulating animality with beasts, and that difficulty is perhaps not without relation to the troubling logicization of an original constituent that, in the final analysis, is not really synonymous with animality.

Three remarks as a conclusion. First of all, it must be repeated that the great Husserlian inauguration of a form of reason that is constituent only in so far as it is itself constituted has, to a certain extent, allowed the animal not to be dispossessed. Second, in spite of the motif of the transcendental, we remain in a Leibnizian world, a world of a scale of beings and therefore of continuism. Third, what had begun so well and has not yet borne fruit must not so much be begun again—because the idea of transcendental life, as difficult as it may be, remains a precious resource against reductionisms, a resource that is both monist and antipositivist—as it must be reworked while paying closer attention to what zoologists and ethologists tell us about the beasts they study and spend time with.

Malebranche, that abominable and fantastic mechanist, had a wonderful expression: reason always has the movement to take itself even further. One is tempted to apply this expression to the generosity that characterizes reason when Aristotle institutes it, when Leibniz and Husserl reinstitute it, and when they take the risk of gradualism, analogy, of the "as" and the "as if." Against Descartes, Leibniz returned to Aristotle; Husserl is Aristotelian and Leibnizian in his own way. They are three figures who resemble one another and whom one can gather together because they each testify to a tempering of the human exception.

6

The Pathetic Pranks
of Bio-Art

On the staircase of the Tower of Victory, there has lived from the beginning of time the A Bao A Qu, which is sensitive to the virtues possessed by human souls. It lives upon the first step in a state of lethargy, and comes to conscious life only when someone climbs the stairs. The vibration of the person as he approaches infuses the creature with life, and an inward light begins to glow within it. At the same time, its body and its virtually translucent skin begin to ripple and stir. When a person climbs the stairs, the A Bao A Qu follows almost on the person's heels, climbing up after him, clinging to the edge of the curved treads worn down by the feet of generations of pilgrims. On each step, the creature's color grows more intense, its form becomes more perfect, and the light that emanates from it shines ever brighter. Proof of the creature's sensitivity is the fact that it achieves its perfect form only when it reaches the topmost step, when the person who has climbed the stairs has become a fully evolved and realized spirit. In all other cases, the A Bao A Qu remains as though paralyzed, midway up the staircase, its body incomplete, its color still undefined, its light unsteady. When it cannot achieve its perfect form, the A Bao A Qu suffers great pain, and its moaning is a barely perceptible murmur similar to the whisper of silk. But when the man or woman that revives the creature is filled with purity, the A Bao A Qu is able to reach the topmost step, completely formed and radiating a clear blue light. Its return to life is brief, however, for when the pilgrim descends the stairs again, the A Bao A Qu rolls down to the first step once more, where, now muted and resembling some faded picture with vague outlines, it awaits the next visitor to the Tower. The creature becomes fully visible only when it reaches the midpoint of the staircase, where the extensions of its body (which, like arms, help it to climb the stairs) take on clear definition. There are those who say that it can see with its entire body, and that its skin feels like that of a peach. Down through all the centuries, the A Bao A Qu has reached perfection only once.

—JORGE LUIS BORGES, *The Book of Imaginary Beings*

There are certain artists that mean to mark the end of the avant-garde by setting up their studios in laboratories and working with geneticists so as to act on the mechanisms of life. Artistically modified organisms, writes Eduardo Kac, one of these artists to whose work I will be paying particular attention, "are going to become our familiar companions."[1] He adds that "artists could usefully increase the planet's biodiversity by inventing new forms of life." For these artists, it is a question of replacing the representation of life with its modification and of exhibiting the results of these *détournements* in museums. For example, a rabbit capable of emitting a green glow thanks to the introduction of a jellyfish gene into his DNA . . .

One might begin by wondering who could claim to know both the history of science and the history of art and be fluent enough in the "two cultures" to have the right to evaluate what is a contradiction in terms: "biological art." Either the audience of these biotechnological installations finds itself infantilized, brought down to the level of experiments usually reserved for children in the discovery centers of science museums where the manipulation of a few controls can produce impressive effects; or else the audience is credited with competencies of which very few among our art gallery visiting contemporaries can boast. This is why it has rightly been said that this is an "art of belief."

Art imitates nature or completes what nature is incapable of doing, one more or less reads in the second book of Aristotle's *Physics*. With its ambiguity, this sentence remains of exemplary pertinence, because at the same time that it institutes our traditional concepts of nature and technique, it also invites us to consider what the artisan fabricates as a paradigm for natural causality; in Ancient Greek, the word *technē* signifies both "manual art" and "work of art." Aristotle nonetheless adds a reservation to this analogy: finality that is extrinsic when it is a question of art is intrinsic when it is a question of nature. And it is on this point that Aristotle's physics have become dated, since both Darwinism and our contemporary "synthetic theory of evolution" teach us that there is no teleology in the history of life but only chance and necessity, both of which are of course compatible with segmental teleonomies. This Aristotelian framework can nonetheless act as a safeguard for those who, when solicited by these "biological arts" seeking recognition, attempt to resist the idiocy of the undertaking.

Yet it is certainly not in the name of Nature, of the Creator God, or of the Art of the Easel or even of an Ethical Committee that I am confronting biological, biotechnological, genetic, and transgenic arts. On the contrary, I am trying to remain Darwinian by considering that innovations and experimentations with limits (between species, between arts and techniques, between men and animals, between the natural and the symbolic) are in no way events, or what we call "events," in the history of men. Not that they have always existed in the way we know them today. How could one deny that, despite progress in bionics, there is still a discontinuity between the technological arts of artificial intelligence and the biotechnological arts, in other words, between silicon and carbon, or between the Aibo dog built by Sony and the florescent dog K9 put together by Eduardo Kac? The genetic and transgenic arts do indeed constitute a deviation, one that represents a new phylogenetic phase. Yet even if they produce something we have never seen before, this only reflects a moment of Evolution that is offering itself for our consideration. Who could still be naïve enough to believe that some inspired free will intervenes in the great process without subject that is the history of life and the discovery of its processes? Artists who participate in this kind of work thus look more like busybodies of epigenesis than outsiders or demiurges. It is as if they were themselves programmed by Evolution as a way of reproducing and spectacularizing certain experimentations in hybridization and transgenesis.

It is axiologically neutral: neither good nor bad, neither beautiful nor ugly.

What is nonetheless disconcerting and may at first be off-putting is the fact that in the Western tradition, despite new scientific paradigms and new techniques, it so happens that the arts have almost always served a very specific function: saying no or saying something else, taking a few steps back or just to one side, effectuating shifts that attest to the fact that the human being is and has, in front of him, an indefinite complexity whose recessive possibilities he can explore by proposing paths other than the path of progress, by expressing melancholy, nostalgia, or revolt, all those negative, politically deviant passions. Quite to the contrary, the biotech artist brings science and art to work with one another in the elaboration of simplistic models that furnish a perception of how the world functions. This only means that the artisans of a synergy between genetics, the Internet, the neurosciences, and the arts under consideration here refuse to offer up any world beyond the technocosmos. For them, it has become a question of collaborating with what is and what inevitably will be. It is no longer a question, except in certain cases, of an exile far away from what no longer is or in close proximity to what is going to disappear; it is also no longer a question of waiting for what may happen, or of encountering the incalculable. This is why one must repeat that these installations, however new they may be, cannot be qualified as *events*.

After this initial reaction, one feels somewhat uneasy when one learns from the artist himself that comments from the audience or from any person who learns, even at a distance, of certain pieces of biological art are treated as an integral part of the work itself. The aesthetico-biological system swallows and absorbs all these reactions, reactions of rejection being no doubt particularly important. This art inscribed in time as a work in progress can therefore inspire reactions of irritation, but it couldn't care less given that under the guise of dialogue, any forms of resistance it inspires are interpreted as predictable symptoms that nourish the system's complexity.

Upon even further reflection, one begins to wonder how the constant recourse these "creators" have to discourse as a way of explaining their intentions can be justified. Does not the swelling of notices and interviews only heighten the prosthetic pompousness? A major ambiguity seems in fact to float over these installations in terms of what the artist expects from his audience. Is his intent, in spite of it all, still aesthetic, or is it merely didactic, or else is it perhaps critical? What is most often said of this work is that it offers a unique opportunity for raising consciousness, and therefore for ethical and democratic debate on the causes and consequences of biotechnologies. What should be made of this? I strongly agree with Jens Hauser when he says that these arts effectuate a *détournement* of utilitarian discourse.[2] And I would go even further: one might think that what we have here in an exaggerated and pathetic form is what Kant called "finality without end," which he maintained was the mode proper to the work of art. Thanks to this playful *détournement,* in effect, we might be said to be freeing ourselves from medical legitimations, from the good humanist word that justifies trial and error, the trials and successes of much of the unrestrained and often cruel research carried out on experimental animals. But in order for this kind of analysis to have the least bit of pertinence, there would have to be a minimal disproportion between, on the hand, the cells and molecules, the DNA sequencing that researchers allow artists to play with, and, on the other, the incommensurable effective possibilities being created in laboratories.

This is why it seems particularly laughable when certain biotech artists invoke how "responsible" they are making us, and claim that their work offers a unique opportunity for ethical debate about chimeras. By inviting us to react in a piously normative way, they prove that they act on the basis of a transcendent, extrinsic justification that might save their entertainment from being pure "art for art's sake" or merely blatant inanity. "There is no transgenic art," says Eduardo Kac, "without a firm commitment to and responsibility for the new life form thus created. . . . The result of transgenic art processes must be healthy creatures capable of as regular a development as any other creatures from related species. These animals are to be loved and nurtured just like any other animal."[3] The benevolence of these statements is somewhat baffling, since adopting a mutt from the Humane Society would be just as good an action, and much cheaper than the costs of transporting a fluorescent Fluffy the bunny from the laboratory in Jouy-en-Josas to an apartment in Chicago. In fact, the ethical dimension of this so-called communicational aesthetic can be reduced to the exchange of messages on the Internet and the triggering of rays of light that encourage the growth or mutation of living matter. Kac criticizes traditional works of art for offering a unidirectional message to spectators and of leaving them "outside the dialogue." With transgenic art, on the other hand, we gain access to dialogic interaction. Since the work implicates other living beings, it becomes unpredictable and cannot be controlled. And this space of dialogue is what the work actually is, not the rabbit itself.

One can begin with the objection that the adjective "conventional" is an abusive generalization that impoverishes painting, starting with Paleolithic rock art and continuing through to Fautrier, Bacon, Rebeyrolle, and Gilles Aillaud. In addition, it is often *in spite of ourselves* that the so-called dialogical genre forces us to collaborate in the work's composition. At any rate, we cannot accept that what is called dialogue be confiscated by electronic messages. As for the "uncontrollable" and "unpredictable" aspect Kac mentions, one can readily concede that these are very big words to name a random process that, in the current state of things, gives little credit to chain reactions.

As a matter of fact, how is it that the only true political problem posed by these installations in which art is used as a kind of surplus value is never addressed? Do the adepts of biotech art condemn the scandal of the biotechnological and pharmaceutical multinational companies that have no goal beyond profit and that implacably push for patenting the living and therefore of turning it into a piece of commercial merchandise like any other? If this question is never addressed within the works themselves, it's probably because, thanks to the media that are constantly talking about them, the petri dishes of these artists offer good publicity to the firms that finance them, allowing them to further develop their market logics. We are at the antipodes of what these "creators" claim about their work: that it is a contribution to a new form of ecology.

I will therefore spend some time on the work of Eduardo Kac, since this artist seems to bring together and totalize the main characteristics of transgenic art and to represent its boldest distinct proposition. One should nonetheless begin by distinguishing between two different kinds of material used in his work; both are genetic but each demands a different kind of analysis. On the one hand, there is the manipulation of the mechanisms of living things, of genetic material, in other words of more or less abstract processes: this is the case in the performance called *Genesis.* On the other hand, there is the manipulation of this same material, but with the effect of changing extremely complex living individuals: this is the case with the Alba rabbit and the K9 dog.

The principle of *Genesis,* a work realized with the help of Charles Strom, consists in the invention of what Kac calls an "artist's gene" that does not exist in nature. Bacteria are genetically modified by this "artist's gene," to which a jellyfish's gene, the GFP protein, is added, thus producing fluorescence. The first part of the performance consists in translating several lines from a text from Genesis widely held as foundational in our culture into Morse code: "Have dominion over the fish of the sea, and over the fowl of the air, and over every living thing that moveth upon the earth."[4] Then Kac transforms the Morse code obtained from the translation into DNA. The synthetic genes of the irradiated plasmids that have been made to mutate either in situ or from a distance by participants and spectators of the work are then taken by lighting an ultraviolet lamp that is part of the installation. The genetic sequence is then retranslated in the opposite direction until it returns to its terminal sentence in a vulgar language.

In the many explanations Eduardo Kac has given of *Genesis,* what is most striking is his insistence on the term "creation." Kac uses this word that no one in art history has dared to use for a long time now—it dates back to Romanticism—to designate the use of genetic material as material when in reality it is merely a parasite of genetic engineering. What he calls "creations" are actually procedures more closely related to coupling apparatuses, assemblages, and recombinations—themselves related to a more or less authorized pirating of genes, to second- or even third-hand knowledge, or scientifically assisted bricolage, artistic practices that could in no way find their model in some kind of inaugural act borrowed from the book of Genesis. This is the case even if, to speak of Eduardo Kac as Eduardo Kac does, one adds an "eighth day" to what emerges *ex machina* and not *ex nihilo.* "Eighth day" is in effect the title of another one of his works that I am citing as a way of underlining a fantasy of monotheistic omnipotence, a laughable desire to rival with what has imposed itself on us for more than three millennia as creation.

Several questions arise about *Genesis* and in particular this one: does Kac believe in the truth of Revelation to the point of making a verse from the Bible proclaiming the domination of man over animals the origin and foundation of our Western relation to beasts? There is much to be said about this received idea, and I would personally be of the opinion that the crucifixion of God made man, in so far as it acts as a substitute for the animal sacrifices common in the Hebraic and Greek religions, is much more decisive.

What language does he read Genesis in? Not in Greek or in Hebrew, the languages of the original, but in English. Why? Is it in the King James Version or in one of those translations one finds in one's nightstand in Protestant countries? I haven't found an answer to this nonetheless decisive question, because of course one does not get the same Morse code, and therefore the same genetic code, and therefore the same bacteria according to the materiality of the signifier being used as the point of departure. In fact, does the passage from a text into Morse code and then into DNA and back again deserve the name "translation"? The translation of a literary text is probably the least mechanical and automatic and most interpretative act there is.

In this linguistico-genetic back and forth, is there not a clearly disconcerting occidental-centrism and a biblical quasi-fundamentalism? In this particular case, it is a matter of "changing God's words," says Kac. He modifies divine prescription and disobeys him, but only by obeying him. At the very least, one can observe in this way of proceeding a theologizing epistemology that brings us straight back to Galilean mechanics, to the paradigm according to which God wrote the text of nature in a mathematical language as a way of allowing us to decipher it.

It seems to me that the manifest content of these actions and of this discourse, in other words the *critique of anthropocentrism* inherent in the unveiling of the porosity of boundaries among living beings, only barely hides their latent content, a classically and laughably Promethean or Faustian *anthropocentrism*, an exorbitant mastery and a demiurgic humanism that appropriates all rights over the living, including the right to exhibit its transmutations as if we were a circus: what Kac calls a "monstration of the invisible." The first two narcissistic wounds mentioned by Freud caused by Copernicus and then by Darwin show themselves to be very poorly healed, or rather cauterized, by the omnipotence of this so-called artistic genius infatuated with genetic engineering.

Eduardo Kac claims that a connection between the scientific, artistic, and religious has always existed, because painters used perspective to represent religious subjects! Can we follow him in this claim to affiliate his innovations with this precedent? I would instead agree with Jens Hauser when he underlines that the biological arts abolish the paradigms of representation and metaphor. This is why I am not pursuing a critique—this is not the space to do so—of the facile transgression constituted by genetic and transgenic practices. What I am trying to call into question, though, and what is related precisely to these issues of representation, is a transgression of transgression that operates on two levels: first, there is a venial violation of the ordinary finality of the laboratory through the mirror and the play of art; second, there is the transgression that seems more serious since it is effectuated on the symbolic level as an offensive against the regime of textuality through the acting out of metaphors and metamorphoses. Freud would have said that this is a case of converting the representation of words into the representation of things that, as is well known, characterizes psychosis.

As for those other "works" by Kac, the Alba rabbit and soon the K9 dog, fluorescent under ultraviolet light thanks to the jellyfish DNA injected into their DNA, these *artistically modified organisms* solicit ethological and ontological questions since these are mammals and living individuals that have been genetically transformed. We do in fact learn that the French army commissioned a fluorescent bull from the INRA.[5] The army ended up having the bull slaughtered: as an artwork or as military material? It so happens that there is nothing new about this technique, since researchers often use it on mice as a way of observing the evolution of proteins. "The fluo rabbit," as Olivier Cadiot wonderfully writes, "is the exact opposite of our classic cows, he's entirely new, fluorescent green hair and whiskers, Fluorescent Green, it could be the name of a rose. Realized with love by a lab artist in his hospital-studio, a living prototype with soft, cloned ears, the ideal target for transparent countryside, a 4D game for a new hunter. Boom."[6]

I do nonetheless acknowledge the fact that by comparing this *work* that consists in introducing an inoffensive mark into the genes of an animal with works by Hermann Nitsch, the Austrian artist who organizes bloody slaughters of cows and sheep, or even with works by Wim Delvoye,[7] who tattoos motifs and shields onto pigs' skin and who, in order to do so, must anesthetize them even though their hearts are extremely fragile, one can at first feel somewhat relieved. At first sight, Kac's artistic practice seems not to be too intrusive, not too aggressive, and in fact he himself has underlined this. Yet there is something obvious here that forces us to ask a few questions: how many trials and failures have there been, that is, how many animal deaths? And what is to become of the GFP-K9 dog, begun in December 2000? And, especially, what has actually become of that Alba destined to be exhibited in a gallery in 2000 during the Avignon numérique festival, Alba who was supposed to be quietly adopted by Eduardo Kac's family and who in the end was placed under house arrest in one of INRA's laboratories. "Support E. Kac's efforts to free Alba and allow her to come home! Write in Alba's Guestbook!" one could read on one of Kac's websites. And what is to be made of this saccharine familialist sentimentalism that oozes through the artist's words when he speaks of the little bunny he holds in his arms and when he reveals the origin of its name, chosen with the help of his wife and daughter? Animals definitely have a right to more respect. They simply have the right to have rights.

A beast attached to a laboratory table for experimentation and manipulated by men with incomprehensible gestures is horrible enough, even when one is aware of the conflicting values at play. But what is to be said of those who accomplish gestures like this with the lamentable goal of making art by creating a fluorescent dog? Behind these playful manipulations, one can make out the old voyeur's mentality, that sinister scopic drive that more or less brought us to parade the Elephant Man about in fairs, to present the Hottentots in a hut at the World Exhibitions, and to place dwarfs on display in the circus. On the other hand, Rembrandt's *Slaughtered Ox,* Chardin's *Jellyfish,* all the carcasses painted by Soutine, Dürer's *Young Hare,* perhaps even Beuys's *How to Explain Pictures to a Dead Hare,* and that flayed horse with his equally flayed rider that Fragonard—not the painter but the anatomist whose works can be seen at Maisons-Alfort—called *The Horseman of the Apocalypse* as a tribute to one of Dürer's engravings, all these still-lifes, all these remains, and even that happening offer themselves to eyes that may be frightened but are never deceived: one could almost say that these works soothe our ruined eyes.

In this context, how can one not think of *Bouvard and Pécuchet,* Flaubert's great epic and cantankerous encyclopedia of inanity? One comic episode comes to my mind. The two friends apply the theories and practical advice they discover in all kinds of manuals of scientific vulgarization in absolutely literal ways. For a while, they are madly interested in magnetism and hypnotism, which were more or less for the 1850s what DNA is in our time. One day, Pécuchet decides to hypnotize the turkeys on a Norman farm by tying up their feet and drawing a bright white line in the middle of the courtyard. He succeeds in hypnotizing the animals, turkey after turkey, until the furious peasants chase him and his companion away.

While conducting an entirely different kind of experiment on a robotic bat called BatBot that he constructed in Rotterdam in 1999, Kac got interested in philosophy. He placed his robot in a colony of real bats installed in an artificial cave in the zoo. Thanks to a virtual reality helmet, the spectator found him- or herself in the middle of the cave and perceived it as bats do, thanks to the visualization of sonar effects. The philosopher Thomas Nagel's question, "What does it feel like to be a bat?" was the inspiration for this experiment that consists in an effort to penetrate into an animal's sensoriality, to put oneself in its position. This representation of the other living being's representation is one of the objects of cognitive ethology, and it is also what has long been called *Einfühlung,* or empathy, in phenomenology. Interviewed by the French newspaper *Le Monde,* Kac declares, "We don't know if a bacteria or a plant has a consciousness, but we have no doubt about the rabbit and the dog."[8] Kac here imagines he has encountered a fundamental idea of phenomenology and ethology. Yet, first, he does not take the time to know what kind of encounter this should be. And second, he is not able to help us understand how the "continued creation" of Alba and K9 would improve empathy between nonhuman living beings and humans: in this case, there seems to be a screaming contradiction between the end and the means.

The disaster consists in the fact that while Kac claims to lend support to his concept of "communicational aesthetics" and to nourish his technological passion for communication between animals and humans, he has either not read or has poorly read the authors he cites. Leaving Descartes to one side, generally known as the theoretician of the animal-machine, who Kac says "has a condescending approach to the spiritual life of the animal," we can go straight to what is most distressing. Kac is constantly confusing interconnection, alterity, intersubjectivity, dialogue, empathy, dialogism, and communicational ethics. The thirty pages he has signed and that can be found on the Internet under the title "GFP Bunny" are incredibly confused.[9] One is stupefied to see the artist equip his essay with an enormous critical apparatus of cut-and-paste quotations that allow him to boast of erudite references, Levinasian thinking of the other, for example, even though despite several moving texts that describe a dog and a camel,[10] it is a constitutive aspect of Levinas's thought to exclude the relation to animals from the experience of alterity. As for Buber, who is also cited by Kac, his problematic of the I and the Thou is hardly fitting for his sentimental and slapdash reveries, since animals have no place in the dialogue between the I and the Thou. This is true even if Buber did happen to write a disturbing piece about the cat.[11]

Let us not even mention the reference to Habermas and the clichés of communicational ethics. Is Kac truly unaware or only pretending to be unaware of the fact that the majority of continental philosophers whose names he cites were only and restrictively interested in human intersubjectivity and that they have always already chased animals away from the common world—and even from their conception of alterity? It was not enough to salute the exception represented by Husserl and Merleau-Ponty. It would have also been necessary for these two decisive authors for thinking about animal reality to be correctly solicited, which is far from being the case since none of their works dealing specifically with animality is cited. This is why I will not resist the desire to recall how phenomenology traced the lineaments of man–animal intersubjectivity, and how this approach is incompatible with the precedents Kac believes support his work.

Even though his rants refer in particular to Husserl, I will be calling upon Merleau-Ponty to furnish this sorcerer's apprentice with a few elementary aspects of phenomenology. In a 1957–58 course at the Collège de France, the philosopher addresses the question of the animal's relation to the word by basing himself on the hierarchy of the species. Entirely planned animals such as sea urchins and jellyfish that are insensitive to stimuli, lacking in environment, and regulated by the external milieu, can be said to be pure processes. On the other hand, animals who plan, protoplasm capable of plasticity (such as an amoeba who makes pseudopods or vacuoles and then makes them disappear in order to recreate them) enact regulations, and dispose of a certain capacity for prediction. Of this phenomenon, Merleau-Ponty goes so far as to say that "we see the protoplasm move, a living matter that moves; to the right, the animal's head, to the left, its tail. From this moment on, the future comes before the present. A field of space-time has been opened: here we have a beast."[12] In this same perspective of a phenomenology of life, Hans Jonas will go so far as to maintain that metabolism is the first level of the emergence of meaning.[13]

Finally, there is a third kind of animal, those that are without plan and that can be called superior. They construct an environment that is replicated in their nervous system. Stimuli are subject to elaboration and are "translated" into the linguistic system of the nervous system that is itself in a way a mirror of the world. Thinking of these animals that are open to the stimuli that solicit them more as signs than as causes, Merleau-Ponty writes, "All zoology presupposes an *Einfühlung* on our part, a methodical empathy with animal behavior, the animal's participation in our perceptive life and our perceptive life's participation in animality."[14]

With more highly evolved vertebrates, one does in effect discover something like the beginning of a subjective interiority, the expression of a self that is constituted by the pursuit of an end, a goal-oriented activity that testifies to strategies of adaptation, which imply a psycho-physiological identity in time. This identity includes mental states, beliefs, desires, emotions, inferences, perception, memory, and anticipation. This is the reason for the incontestable reality of anxieties and frustrations. It is also why certain animals go insane, as studied by a French psychiatrist named Henri F. Ellenberger.[15] This is also why recourse to anxiolytics and even to genetic manipulations has been taken as a way of abolishing the nervous tension due to industrial methods of intensive breeding, seclusion in zoos, and animal experimentation.

This is why when confronted with the manipulations of bio-art, one has to emphasize the phenomenological pertinence of the three R's that researchers, including researchers at the INRA, have proposed and that could constitute a deontology for laboratories concerning beings endowed with sensibility and worlds.[16] Three rules. When possible, *replacement,* which consists in substituting nonsentient species for sentient ones or in carrying out experiments in vitro. When replacement is not possible, *reduction,* which consists in limiting experiments on sentient animals to experiments that are considered indispensible. And finally, *refinement,* which aims to reduce any inflicted suffering as much as possible. One will note that the geneticist who contributed to the "creation" of a fluorescent rabbit unfortunately broke the first two of these rules in a shocking way.

Kac cannot legitimately claim to have inherited anything from the lessons of phenomenologists and ethologists for whom the animal is quite precisely not a part of nature but a particular relation to the world. For this would imply acknowledging that the animal has an inherent or intrinsic value and that it should therefore never be treated merely as a means or as material, as a sample for postmodern experimentation. This is why I placed this reflection on transgenic arts under the protection of a text by Borges. Do I hear you saying that it's pretty much the same thing? No! Quite to the contrary! For A Bao A Qu's light, the one that shines from literature, gives us the strength to refuse without reservation the production and exhibition of Alba's and K9's and to take immense pity on the poor living detritus of a techno-science in the clutches of debauchery.

7

The Ordinariness of Barbarity

But if instinct does, in fact, signify man's indisputable animal nature, it is not at all clear why this animal nature should be less docile when it is embodied in a reasonable being. The form of the adage, *homo homini lupus,* deceives us as to its meaning, and Baltasar Gracian, in a chapter of his *Criticòn* (*The Critick*), constructs a fable in which he shows what the moralist tradition means when it says that man's ferocity toward his semblable exceeds everything animals are capable of, and that carnivores themselves recoil in horror at the threat man poses to nature as a whole.

—JACQUES LACAN, *Ecrits*

In Latin, *crudelitas* designated cruelty only when it coincided with *cruor,* spilled blood, whether coagulated or in a puddle, wounded flesh. As for noble blood, it was called *sanguis.* This is why the consecrated phrase is "Hic est enim calix sanguinis mei." This observation is less incongruous than it might at first appear, since this divine blood was in no way shed for any kind of redemption of the animals, and since this is precisely the *crucial* characteristic of our Western Christian culture. This semantic remark must nonetheless not allow us to ignore the fact that one can act with extreme physical cruelty without any blood being shed at all.

And if we now look at synonyms with a sustained attention to their etymology, we discover that cruelty consists in behaving with *ferocity,* in other words like a ferocious beast, *ferox,* or *savagely,* like a nondomestic animal, or *barbarously,* in other words like a uncivilized man, or else with *inhumanity,* for language obliges us to say that a man does not deserve his place in the human race when he shows signs of cruelty: if we often lapse into the anthropomorphism that consists in deploring nature's cruelty, is this not in effect to accentuate the human exception, given that men are capable of absolute *humanity* even as they are also prone to the infinite enjoyment of evil?[1]

But in this case, what, and perhaps we should say who, are we leaving to suffer, or are we making suffer, when we are cruel with an animal? It is of course still a question of a living being, but the question needs to be more precise: is cruelty toward animals a particular case of general cruelty, or does it have some distinguishing characteristic? One will concede that it all depends on the establishment or the erasure of a border between men and beasts: an interminable prejudicial question that involves the entirety of the philosophical tradition and that I believe I have contributed to treating.[2]

The cruelty one immediately thinks of and about which everyone seems to be in agreement is the pure cruelty of making or allowing suffering for pleasure: an exercise in omnipotence on a sentient being entirely given over to the whims of a subjectivity, physical enjoyment, a *Schadenfreude* proper to man. Childish cruelty toward animals or toward weaker children displays this cruelty. For thinking that would like to believe it is free of belief in original sin and of the thinking of radical evil, it represents such a painful enigma that a materialist eighteenth-century philosopher, Helvetius, confessed that he felt profoundly disturbed when he was faced with children that "enclose chaffers and horn-beetles in hot wax, then dress them up like soldiers, and thus prolong their misery for two or three months."[3]

But we are insisting on the enigma of ontological meanness perhaps only because there is a refusal to see that cruelty toward beasts is the most widespread and most commonly denied thing in the world: it is a banal, quotidian, and legal form of violence, the violence of atrocities not punishable by law. For as things currently stand, it is no longer only death that constitutes the most atrocious violation for an animal, but the enclosure of its poor body and its poor life in the terrifying abstraction of the pet store and the laboratory, or in the concentration-like space of factory farming. The amnesia constitutive of the reality of our ordinary practices and the daily cruelty that inheres in these practices bears a very simple name: indifference. We are not blood-thirsty and sadistic, we are indifferent, passive, blasé, detached, insouciant, hardened, vaguely a party to what is going on, full of good humanist conscience, and we are made this way by the implacable collusion of monotheistic culture, techno-science, and economic imperatives. Yet again, the fact of knowing now what it is others do for us, of not being informed, far from constituting an excuse, represents an aggravating circumstance for the beings endowed with consciousness and the capacity for memory, imagination, and responsibility that we rightly claim to be.

These are the years of mad cow disease and BSE, of infected birds and SARS, of great fear of interspecies contamination, of massive massacres of mammals and birds since we must above all take care of men . . . For they would have us believe that it is not commercial interests and the global licentiousness in development that provokes these new "plagues" of an Egypt that now covers the entire earth. By rationalizing breeding with the goal of maximizing profits, zoo-technology has broken a contract that is not natural, but domestic and tacit, a contract that united us to those among the animals that our distant ancestors had domesticated. It has broken the forms of sociability and hierarchy that characterized the life of traditional farms, when "mixed communities" still existed and services, information, and affects were exchanged, when mutual apprenticeships took place.[4] When we say that cows have gone "mad," are we not also admitting that they cannot be reduced to their metabolic function? Catherine and Raphaël Larrère have shown that by considering living beings as a mere production tool according to the criteria of technology and economy, we have in practice, if not in ontology, arrived at "animal-machines."[5] The worst of it is therefore hidden in the incredible hypocrisy of advising and putting into practice a so-called "ethics of well-being," as if it were a question of being motivated enough by respect for animals to place limitations on industrial breeding's acts of brutality when industry necessarily makes money off of the proper functioning and profitability of the business.[6] If the integrity of a living being is defined by the coherence of its progressive development, it therefore concerns the individual as well as the species and the variety, and should thus require that the trauma and lasting intrusion of heteronomy not be inflicted upon it.

Policies of slaughter whose impetus is the fear of epizootics, and particularly of bovine spongiform encephalopathy due to a herbivore's ingestion of meat and bone meal, have therefore been elegantly popularized under the name of "the mad cow crisis": probably as a way of not having to point at the madmen that *we* have become. In these diseases transmitted to man under the name of Creutzfeldt-Jakob disease and with heightened and severe respiratory symptoms, contagion brazenly transgresses the interspecies barrier. The indifference and cowardly relief of the consent given to ever-increasing slaughter underline a brutality that has nothing bestial about it—even if in Latin, animals are called *animalia bruta.* Is it really a sign of stubborn antihumanism to be shocked by the way world leaders and international media insist exclusively on problems of public health without a care for the cruel and absurd destiny of these beasts massively destroyed and burned at the stake? We are far too often besieged by complacent images and drawings of bovines struck with the erratic behavior so many mock, then with dead animals, pulled by cranes, completely disarticulated, still in one piece but grotesquely deformed, their tongues wagging and their eyes askew, as if the victims of these disasters were photographed at a wide angle. When Rembrandt and Soutine painted a slaughtered cow or a section of beef, they expressed, as I have said, the piety and pity of art for those who are dismembered so that men can be fed on them. But today, our images render the immemorial relation and strong and deep symbolic link that ties man to the domestic animal null and void.

The civilizations from which we hail performed sacrifices: an always perfectly healthy animal was offered to a god or to the gods. A part of it was burned in homage to the divinity, and the other part of it was eaten. Sometimes the entire animal was burned, and this was called a "holocaust." This is the very thing we think we are performing in these massacres, while in fact, quite unlike these ancient rituals, the "destroyed" animals are sick or presumed to be sick and the divine no longer exists: the god we honor reigns over the services of meat and poultry producers, and therefore over the sacred plate of the consumer. Using another false analogy with Antiquity, it is a euphemism to speak of a "hecatomb"; what this term named was the sacrificial slaughter of a hundred cows. The numbers do not match when this word is used to speak of the extermination of millions of farm-bred animals.

Political decision-makers have obeyed a logic of public health that coincides with the breeders' submission to the economic logic that consists, at moments of crisis in the market, of getting rich off of slaughter. Behind this sinister coherence, we find something of a perfectly cynical rationality. Confronted with this barely imaginable contradiction—one that democratic policies, founded on their projection into the future, on advanced planning and progress, could not predict and even actively contributed to provoking such a danger for their populations—those who govern us resign themselves to archaic and almost magical behavior. They repeat these simulacra of holocausts as if to expiate the crime that consists in treating the birth, life, and death of these living beings in no more than an industrial way, living beings that are not things that could survive a submission to all that was doled out by the whims of a stubborn anthropocentrism.[7]

Industrial slaughter has already turned administered bloodbaths into a purely technical act. But the absurdity of the calculations of profitability becomes abundantly clear when animals are massacred for nothing: just so that we do not eat them. This productivist, technical, and commercial civilization, one that calls itself *humanist* yet is forgetful of the amphibology of the word "culture" and forgetful in particular of the living being the animal is, is what has made these bloody exhibits possible, if not necessary.

The principle of precaution has itself gone mad. Probably for political reasons, it has been taken to such a radical extreme that it has become excessive. Why, for example, do we need to slaughter herds affected by the good old foot-and-mouth disease of our country, since this disease is not mortal and does not contaminate man? Are we not being inconsequential by being overly cautious, in the same way that the food industry is? The principle of precaution is gradually killing beasts and could potentially kill them interminably. In both cases—of production and precaution—we are acting irresponsibly with animals that are in our care, but also, in a less immediate way, with men who are in our care.

For these scenes of extermination can have consequences that, on the symbolic level, will turn out to be destructuring and dehumanizing. Priority should of course be given to the health of human beings, but it is not enough to take care of bodies; we must also be aware of our representations and of our actions around life and death. These animal existences interrupted at a pure loss reveal to everyone, and in particular to children, the fact that our model of industrialization of the living is fundamentally nihilistic, that we are polluting death without even noticing it. And if one makes the effort to follow the chain of causality, one will quickly understand that from the massive destruction that allows us to avoid eating to slaughter that allows us to eat, to industrial farming and finally to breeding practiced as mode of production among others, the chain is unbroken. If we blithely persist in this brazenly increasing technicization, it would no doubt be simpler to completely and definitively eliminate from our existences all relation with the impure, anguishing, and marvelous effervescence of life in living beings.

Before it is too late, we must therefore cease opposing subjective, powerless, and particular pity with objective, universal, and efficient law, and the animal question must once again become a social question, just as it was for Michelet and for Hugo, who, as progressive men, demanded that the borders of the city-state be stretched wide enough to welcome beasts within them. One will never repeat enough that it is in the name of the republic and of democracy that, against the Catholic and conservative right wing, they tirelessly defended the right of our "inferior brothers" not to suffer for nothing. They made it clear that the stakes of this struggle were political, because it concerned the life of men. We must acknowledge the fact that what we do to all living beings endowed with sensitivity and worlds are things we do to ourselves. Biology, genetics, and the theory of evolution teach us that continuity and kinship (which is patent even if intolerable to some) befall all guests on the earth. The time is ripe for the status of animals, and most urgently of farm-bred animals, otherwise known as livestock, to find a place in international law that facilitates the existence of a community of the living that can counter human omnipotence and the horrible fraternity of contamination. These legal reforms can only be undertaken if the meaning of pity is reevaluated. The philosophical and political war over this subject has no doubt never been entirely quiet, but today, it has entered into a critical phase. "To think the war we find ourselves waging is not only a duty, a responsibility, an obligation, it is also a necessity, a constraint that, like it or not, directly or indirectly, no one can escape. Henceforth more than ever. . . . The animal looks at us, and we are naked before it. Thinking perhaps begins here."[8]

Notes

PREFACE

1. Elisabeth de Fontenay, *Le silence des bêtes: La philosophie à l'épreuve de l'animalité* (Paris: Fayard, 1998).

2. Sigmund Freud, *Inhibitions, Symptom, Anxiety,* trans. James Strachey (New York: W. W. Norton, 1990), 62, 84.

3. [English-language readers may be jarred by Fontenay's repeated use of the word "man" (*homme*) when she writes about the difference between humans and animals. The use of this masculine signifier to speak of humanity seems to indicate something of the extent of her critical attachment to a philosophical tradition of "what is proper to man." I have decided to follow the gender-specificity of Fontenay's term because of its resonance in the philosophical tradition she engages.—Trans.]

4. Jorge Luis Borges with Margarita Guerrero, *The Book of Imaginary Beings,* trans. Andrew Hurley (New York: Viking, 2005), 83.

5. Denis Diderot, *D'Alembert's Dream,* trans. Leonard Tancock (New York: Penguin Classics, 1976), "Sequel to the Conversation," 226.

6. Arthur Rimbaud, *Illuminations,* trans. Louise Varèse (New York: New Directions, 1946), xxxi–xxxii.

I. THEIR SECRET ELECT

1. Jacques Derrida and Elisabeth Roudinesco, *For What Tomorrow,* trans. Jeff Fort (Stanford: Stanford University Press, 2004).

2. Jacques Derrida, *The Animal That Therefore I Am,* ed. Marie-Louise Mallet, trans. David Wills (New York: Fordham University Press, 2008), 18. Only the introduction to a series of four seminars given over the course of about ten hours in 1997, during a conference at Cerisy-la-Salle,

had appeared in 1997 in the acts to the colloquium "The Autobiograph-
ical Animal." The second part of the seminar, which figures in *The Animal
That Therefore I Am,* appeared under the title "Et si l'animal répondait?"
("And what if the animal responded?"), in *Cahiers Jacques Derrida* 83, ed.
Marie-Louise Mallet and Ginette Michaud (Paris: L'Herne, 2004).

3. Derrida, *The Animal That Therefore I Am,* 30.

4. Ibid., 3.

5. "'Eating Well,' or the Calculation of the Subject," in *Points . . . :
Interviews, 1974–1994,* ed. Elisabeth Weber, trans. Peter Connor and
Avital Ronell (Stanford: Stanford University Press, 1995), 255–87.

6. Derrida, "What Is Poetry" ["Che cos'è la poesia?"], in *Points . . . ,*
trans. Peggy Kamuf, 297.

7. Derrida, *The Animal That Therefore I Am,* 297.

8. Ibid., 7.

9. Derrida, "Istrice 2: Ick bünn all hier," in *Points . . . ,* trans. Peggy
Kamuf, 303.

10. Martin Heidegger, *Identity and Difference,* trans. Joan Stambaugh,
(Chicago: University of Chicago Press, 2002).

11. Derrida, *Points,* 303.

12. Ibid.

13. *Ereignis,* a German word proper to Heideggerian vocabulary, is
commonly translated as "event."

14. Derrida, *Points,* 312.

15. Ibid.

16. Derrida, *The Animal That Therefore I Am,* 4.

17. In a poem I was unable to find, Vigny evokes a woman's reaction
of sudden modesty when her dog sees her undress. Gaston Bachelard
alludes to this poem in *Poétique de la reverie* (Paris: PUF, 1971), 160.

18. Derrida, *The Animal That Therefore I Am,* 3.

19. Walter Benjamin, "On Language as Such and on the Language of
Man," trans. Edmund Jephcott, in *Selected Writings,* vol. 1, ed. Marcus
Bullock and Michael W. Jennings (Cambridge, Mass.: Harvard Univer-
sity Press, 1996), 62–74.

20. Derrida, *The Animal That Therefore I Am,* 16.

21. Ibid., 17.

22. Ibid., 28.

23. Ibid., 32.

24. Ibid., 18.

25. Ibid., 15.

26. Martin Jay, *The Dialectical Imagination* (Berkeley: University of California Press, 1996), 256.

27. Derrida, *The Animal That Therefore I Am,* 19.

28. Ibid., 25.

29. See Jacques Derrida, *D'un ton apocalyptique adopté naguère en philosophie* (Paris: Galilée, 1983).

30. Derrida, *The Animal That Therefore I Am,* 26.

31. Ibid., 12.

32. Ibid., 26.

33. Ibid.

34. Isaac Bashevis Singer, "The Letter Writer," in *Collected Stories: "Gimpel the Fool" to "The Letter Writer"* (New York: Library of America, 2004), 750.

35. Derrida, *The Animal That Therefore I Am,* 80.

36. Ibid., 42.

37. Ibid., 91.

38. Derrida, *Points,* 278.

39. Ibid., 283.

40. Ibid., 279.

41. Derrida, *The Animal That Therefore I Am,* 102.

42. Françoise Armengaud seems to concur with the Derridean position. See "Au titre du sacrifice: L'exploitation économique, symbolique et idéologique des animaux," in *Si les lions pouvaient parler,* ed. Boris Cyrulnik (Paris: Gallimard, 1998), 878.

43. Derrida, *The Animal That Therefore I Am,* 100.

44. Ibid., 100.

45. Ibid., 101.

46. Ibid., 102–3.

47. Ibid., 103.

48. Must we note the fact that, in the Muslim religion, there are no altars?

49. Derrida, *The Animal That Therefore I Am,* 10.

2. The Improper

1. Cf. Jacques Derrida, *Of Spirit: Heidegger and the Question,* trans. Geoffrey Bennington and Rachel Bowlby (Chicago: University of Chicago Press, 1991).

2. Claude Banckaert, *La culture est-elle naturelle?* (Paris: Editions Errance, 1998), 18–19.

3. Cf. the work of Michel Foucault, Jean-François Lyotard, and Jacques Derrida.

4. Frans de Waal, *Good Natured: The Origins of Right and Wrong in Humans and Other Animals* (Cambridge, Mass.: Harvard University Press, 1997).

5. Jean-Pierre Changeux and Paul Ricoeur, *What Makes Us Think?: A Neuroscientist and a Philosopher Argue about Ethics, Human Nature, and the Brain,* trans. M. B. DeBevoise (Princeton: Princeton University Press, 2002), 199.

6. Patrick Tort, *Pour Darwin* (Paris: PUF, 1997).

7. Jean-Marie Schaeffer, *La fin de l'exception humaine* (Paris: Gallimard, 2007).

8. Philippe Descola, *Par-delà nature et culture* (Paris: Gallimard, 2005).

9. Primo Levi, *If This Is a Man,* trans. Stuart Wolf (Abacus, 1958).

10. Genesis 1:26.

11. Sophocles, *Antigone,* 5:332–75.

12. Martin Heidegger, *Introduction to Metaphysics,* trans. Gregory Fried and Richard Polt (New Haven: Yale University Press, 2000), 156–58.

13. Hans Jonas, *The Imperative of Responsibility: In Search of an Ethics for the Technological Age,* trans. Hans Jonas and David Herr (Chicago: University of Chicago Press, 1984).

14. Aristotle, *The Politics* and *The Constitution of Athens,* ed. Stephen Everson (Cambridge: Cambridge University Press, 1996), 13.

15. Plato, Protagoras, 322b.

16. [Fontenay notes that the more habitual French translation for the Greek word *aidōs* is *pudeur,* or modesty—Trans.]

17. Montaigne, *Essays,* 2:12.

18. *Les Cyniques grecs. Fragments et témoignages,* ed. L. Paquet (Ottawa: University of Ottawa Press, 1988) §38, 70–71. [All translations for texts not available in English are by the translator unless otherwise credited—Trans.]

19. Plato, *The Statesman*, ed. Julia Annas and Robin Waterfield (Cambridge: Cambridge University Press, 1995), 262a–63e.

20. Here, I am using Jean-Louis Poirier's analysis in the special edition of *Critique* on "Animalité," August–September 1978.

21. Immauel Kant, *Lectures on Logic,* trans. J. Michael Young (Cambridge: Cambridge University Press, 2004), 538.

22. Immanuel Kant, *Anthropology from a Pragmatic Point of View,* trans. and ed. Robert B. Louden, intro. Manfred Kuehn (Cambridge: Cambridge University Press, 2006) 233, note b.

23. Giovanni Pico della Mirandola, *Oration on the Dignity of Man,* trans. A. Robert Caponigri, intro. Russell Kirk (Los Angeles: Gateway Editions, Inc., 1956) 3.

24. Jean-Jacques Rousseau, *Julie, or the New Heloise,* trans. and annot. Philip Stewart and Jean Vaché (Hanover, N.H.: University Press of New England, 1997), 7.

25. Jean-Paul Sartre, *Existentialism Is a Humanism,* trans. Carol Macomber (New Haven: Yale University Press, 2007); Martin Heidegger, "Letter on Humanism," in *Basic Writings,* ed. David Farrel Krell (New York: Harper Perennial Classics, 2008), 213–66.

26. *Manifeste du cercle de Vienne et autres écrits,* ed. Antonia Soulez (Paris: PUF, 1985), 155–80. In Schaeffer's *La fin de l'exception humaine,* one finds the same hatred of philosophy, argued from an exclusively naturalist-cognitivist point of view.

27. Friedrich Nietzsche, *Daybreak,* ed. Maudemarie Clark and Brian Leiter (Cambridge: Cambridge University Press, 1997), 61.

28. Friedrich Nietzsche, *Fragments Posthumes* (Paris: Gallimard, 1979), 12:294, and *Fragments Posthumes* (Paris: Gallimard, 1977), 14:102.

29. Friedrich Nietzsche, *Fragments Posthumes* (Paris: Gallimard, 1976), 13:79.

30. Friedrich Nietzsche, *Gay Science,* trans. Josefine Nauckhoff and Adrian Del Caro (Cambridge: Cambridge University Press, 2001), 218.

31. Friedrich Nietzsche, *The Wanderer and His Shadow,* § 14, in *Human, All Too Human,* trans. R. J. Hollingdale (Cambridge: Cambridge University Press, 1986), 307.

32. Nietzsche, *Human, All Too Human,* 117.

33. Nietzsche, *The Wanderer and His Shadow,* §14

34. Friedrich Nietzsche, *The Twilight of the Idols* and *The Antichrist,* trans. R. J. Hollingdale (London: Penguin, 1990), 136.

35. Friedrich Nietzsche, *Beyond Good and Evil,* trans. Judith Norman (Cambridge: Cambridge University Press, 2001), 56. [Translation slightly modified—Trans.]

36. Ernst Cassirer, *An Essay on Man* (New Haven: Yale University Press, 1972).

37. Martin Heidegger, *Kant and the Problem of Metaphysics,* trans. Richard Taft (Bloomington: Indiana University Press, 1997).

38. Claude Lévi-Strauss, *The Elementary Structures of Kinship* (Boston: Beacon, 1971).

39. Patrice Maniglier, "L'humanisme interminable de Claude Lévi-Strauss," *Les temps modernes,* no. 609 (June–July–August 2000): 176–215.

40. Michel Tort, "Quelques conséquences de la différence psychanalytique des sexes," *Les temps modernes,* no. 609 (June–July–August 2000): 176–215, and *Fin du dogme paternel* (Paris: Aubier, 2005). See also Monique David-Ménard, "Un vrai débat concernant la psychanalyse," *Les temps modernes,* no. 635–36 (November–December 2005–January 2006): 337–47.

41. Maurice Merleau-Ponty, *Nature: Course Notes from the Collège de France,* comp. Dominique Séglard, trans. Robert Vallier (Evanston, Ill.: Northwestern University Press, 2003), 190.

42. Ibid., 190.

43. Ibid., 198.

44. Ibid., 178.

45. Ibid.

46. Montaigne, *Essays,* 1:42.

47. Descartes, *Discourse on Method* (1637), sec. 5.

48. Derrida, *The Animal That Therefore I Am*, 30.

49. In *The Animal That Therefore I Am,* 29–30, Derrida underlines that he in no way denies an abyssal difference between men and animals.

50. [I am borrowing David Wills's translation of *bêtise* as "asinanity" here, which recuperates at least a portion of the sense of the untranslatable pun between beastliness and stupidity found in the word *bêtise*.—Trans.]

51. This is what researchers in cognitive science call the "theory of mind."

52. On this reading of Aristotle by Jean-Louis Labarrière, "De la phronèsis animale," in *Biologie, logique et métaphysique chez Aristote,* pub. Daniel Devereux and Pierre Pellegrin, Acts of the seminar CNRS-NSF (Paris: Editions du CNRS, 1990).

53. Erich Fried, "Definition," in *Warngedichte* (Frankfurt: Fischer Taschenbuch Verlag, 1984), 134.

54. Maurice Godelier, "Quelle culture pour quels primates?" in Banckaert, *La culture est-elle naturelle?*, 220–21.

55. Christophe Boetsch, "Teaching among Young Chimpanzees," *Animal Behaviour* 41 (1991): 530–32.

56. Frédéric Joulian, "Le casse-noix du chimpanzee: Lectures anthropologique d'un objet simien," in Banckaert, *La culture est-elle naturelle?* 115–37.

57. Frans de Waal, *Peacemaking among Primates* (Cambridge, Mass.: Harvard University Press, 1990), and *Good Natured*.

58. Karl Marx (with Friedrich Engels), *The German Ideology: Including Theses on Feuerbach and Introduction to The Critique of Political Economy*, trans. W. Lough (Amherst, N.Y.: Prometheus Books, 1998), 37.

59. Changeux and Ricoeur, *What Makes Us Think?* 232.

60. Ernst Haeckel, *Anthropogenie* (1874), and *The History of Creation* (1876).

61. Stephen Jay Gould, *The Mismeasure of Man* (New York: W. W. Norton, 1996), 164–65.

62. Hannah Arendt, *On the Origins of Totalitarianism* (New York: Mariner, 1968), 177.

63. René Descartes, *Principles of Philosophy* (1644), 1: § 71.

64. Giorgio Agamben, *The Idea of Prose,* trans. Michael Sullivan and Sam Whitsitt (Albany: State University of New York Press, 1995), 96–97.

3. Between Possessions and Persons

1. Claude Lévi-Strauss, *Le regard éloigné* (Paris: Plon, 1983), 374.

2. Friedrich Engels, *Dialectics of Nature,* trans. and ed. Clemens Dutt (New York: International Publishers, 1940), 17–18.

3. Martin Heidegger, *What Is Called Thinking?* trans. J. Glenn Gray (New York: Harper & Row, 1968).

4. In the *Manuscripts of 1844* for example.

5. Paola Cavalieri, "Les droits de l'homme pour les grands singes non humains," *Le Débat,* no. 108 (January–February 2000). Cladistics is a method of classification of living beings according to their evolutionary ancestry.

6. Jonas, *The Imperative of Responsibility*; Ernst Bloch, *The Principle of Hope,* trans. Neville Plaice, Stephen Plaice and Paul Knight (Cambridge: MIT Press, 1995).

7. We know that women have been particularly active in research on the great apes. See *Grands Singes, Autrement,* 1998, 77–102.

8. Peter Singer, *Animal Liberation* (New York: Ecco, 2002), and *Practical Ethics* (Cambridge: Cambridge University Press, 1993).

9. Mireille Delmas-Marty, in *Du corps humain à la dignité de la personne humaine,* ed. C. Ambroselli and G. Wormser (Paris: Centre national de documentation pédagogique, 1999).

10. It is on the basis of *Animal Liberation* and of Jean-Yves Goffi's book, *Le philosophe et ses animaux* (Nîmes: Jacqueline Chambon, 1994), 191–92, that I present this summary of Peter Singer's theory, which also takes into account the third chapter ("Equality for Animals?") of his *Practical Ethics.*

11. On both of these authors, see Jean-Yves Goffi, *Le philosophe et ses animaux,* 193–216, 93–107, 161–63.

12. Peter Singer, *Animal Liberation,* 8.

13. Ibid., 16, 18.

14. Ibid., 19.

15. Ibid., 20.

16. Peter Singer, *Practical Ethics,* 67.

17. Rapport Micaux, Paris, La documentation française, 1980, 87, quoted by Paul Yonnet in *Le débat,* no. 27 (November 1987).

18. An awkward casuistry: Plutarch, Montaigne, and Locke addressed this theme with greater vivacity and human respect.

19. What insouciance on the part of a philosopher in relation to the complex Greek provenance of this concept of *oikeiōsis* (alliance or appropriation) that Aristotle used to deny the community of the living, Theophrastis to affirm it and the Stoics to name the animal's familiarity with itself.

20. See Fontenay, *Le silence des bêtes,* chap. 1. See also the work of Boris Cyrulnik.

21. This is Heidegger's hypothesis in *The Fundamental Concepts of Metaphysics.*

22. Singer, *Practical Ethics,* 66.

23. Luc Ferry, *The New Ecological Order,* trans. Carol Volk (Chicago: University of Chicago Press, 1995).

24. See Elisabeth Hardouin-Fugier, "Un recyclage français de la propogande nazie: La protection législative de l'animal," *Ecologie politique,* no. 24 (January 2002): 53–70.

25. Georges Canguilhem, *The Knowledge of Life,* ed. Paola Marrati and Todd Meyers, trans. Stefanos Geroulanos and Daniela Ginsburg (New York: Fordham University Press, 2008), 21.

26. Claude Bernard, *Introduction to the Study of Experimental Medicine,* trans. Henry C. Greene (Mineola, N.Y.: Dover Publications, 1957). In the first chapter of the second part of his book, Claude Bernard expansively legitimates animal experimentation in the name of the inviolability of the living human.

27. Singer, *Practical Ethics,* 77.

28. See Fontenay, *Le silence des bêtes,* chap. 19.

29. Jean-Jacques Rousseau, "Discourse on the Origin of Inequality," in *Basic Political Writings,* trans. Donald A. Cress (Indianapolis: Hackett, 1987), 50–52.

30. Jean-Pierre Marguénaud (director of the Observatoire des mutations institutionnelles et juridiques [Observatory of Institutional and Juridical Change], OMJ, Limoges), in an article I will discuss later, shows that French legislation is less empty than some people think. But is it step by step and, as Mireille Delmas-Marty recommends, following the example of Vieira da Silva, that one should legislate (see Ambroselli and Wormser, ed., *Du corps humain à la dignité de la personne humaine*), or is it through the implementation of veritable changes that a coherent and consequential set of rights will be established?

31. I reproduced it as an annex to Plutarch, *Trois traités pour les animaux* (Paris: POL, 1992).

32. Derrida, *The Animal That Therefore I Am,* 87.

33. Cf. the analyses bearing on this question in Florence Burgar, *Animal, mon prochain* (Paris: Odile Jacob, 1997), 31–56.

34. "Deconstruction is a systematic subversion of European metaphysics and an attempt to dissociate critical thought from the institutionalized philosophical tradition," writes Pierre V. Zima in *La Déconstruction* (Paris: PUF, 1994), 7.

35. Walter Benjamin, "Central Park," trans. Edmund Jephcott and Howard Eiland, in *Selected Writings,* vol. 4, ed. Michael W. Jennings (Cambridge, Mass.: Harvard University Press, 2003), 165.

36. Walter Benjamin, "On the Concept of History," trans. Harry Zohn, in ibid. 392.

37. See Max Horkheimer and Theodor W. Adorno, *The Dialectic of Enlightenment,* trans. John Cumming (New York: Continuum, 1972).

38. Fontenay, *Le silence des bêtes,* chap. 4.

39. Goffi, *Le philosophe et les animaux.*

40. A reference to Spinoza, for whom the *conatus* is the tendency a being has to persevere in the being proper to it.

41. See Goffi, *Le philosophe et ses animaux,* 96–107, 161–63.

42. Jean-Claude Nouët and Georges Chapouthier, eds., *Humanité, animalité: Quelles frontières?* (Paris: Connaissances et savoirs, 2006), 85.

43. Ibid., 115.

44. Ibid., 119.

45. Jean-Pierre Marguénaud, "La personnalité juridique des animaux," *Bulletin juridique international pour la protection des animaux (BJAPA) et Recueil Dalloz* 20, special issue devoted to the legal personality of animals, (1998): 205.

46. Ibid.

47. In a collection called *Des animaux et des hommes* (Paris: LGF, 1994), Luc Ferry and Claudine Germé reproduced texts that showed the evolution of French legislation since the Grammont law.

48. Marguénaud, "La personnalité."

49. An article by Yann Thomas, "Le sujet de droit, la personne et la nature," appeared in *Le débat,* no. 100 (May–August 1998), and addressed this problem.

50. Diderot, *D'Alembert's Dream,* trans. Leonard Tancock (New York: Penguin Classics, 1976).

4. RHETORICS OF DEHUMANIZATION

1. *Les juifs rois de l'époque: Histoire de la féodalité financière* (Paris: Librairie de l'Ecole sociétaire, 1845); *L'esprit des bêtes,* 3 vols. (Paris: Librairie Phalanstérienne, 1853–55). [Fontenay's text cites Toussenel's original text in the three-volume edition published in Paris by the Librairie Phalanstérienne. As far as I have been able to tell from my research, only one volume of this book was translated and, interestingly, the anti-Semitic passages that concern Fontenay later in this chapter were omitted from the English (*Passional Zoology: Spirit of the Beasts of France,* translated by M. Edgeworth Lazarus, M.D. [New York: Fowlers and Wells, 1852]). I will therefore be relying on this translation when the passages cited by Fontenay are found in it, with occasional modifications.—Trans.]

2. Marie-Claude Payeur, "L'animal au service de la représentation," *Corpus* no. 16–17 (Paris: Fayard), 29.

3. Ibid.

4. See *La physionomie humaine comparée à la physionomie des animaux d'après les dessins de Charles Le Brun,* commentary L. Métiver (Paris: Renouard-Laurens, 1927). See also Lavater, *Essays on Physiognomy; For the Promotion of the Knowledge and the Love of Mankind,* 3 volumes, trans. Thomas Holcroft (London: G. G. J. and J. Robinson, 1779), or the French translation of the same work, *La Physiognomonie ou l'art de connaître les hommes d'après les traits de leur physionomie* (Lausanne: L'Age d'homme, 1998), 19–218. Both French works include reproductions of drawings by Porta.

5. Diderot, "Sequel to the Conversation," in *D'Alembert's Dream,* trans. Leonard Tancock (New York: Penguin Classics, 1976), 225–34.

6. Pierre Louis Moreau de Maupertuis, *La Vénus physique* (Paris: Aubier-Montaigne, 1980).

7. Claude Lévi-Strauss, *Anthropologie structural 1* (Paris: Plon, 1978).

8. Cf. Michèle Duchet, *Anthropologie et histoire au siècle des Lumières* (Paris: Maspero, 1971), 229–80.

9. Buffon, *De l'homme,* presented by M. Duchet (Paris: Maspero, 1971), 270.

10. Ibid., 223, 226.

11. Ibid., 270.

12. Jean-Jacques Rousseau, *Discourse on the Origins of Inequality,* trans. Franklin Philip, ed. Patrick Coleman (Oxford: Oxford University Press, 1994), 108–9.

13. Ibid. [Translation slightly modified—Trans.]

14. Lavater, *Essays on Physiognomy: For the Promotion of the Knowledge and the Love of Mankind,* trans. Thomas Holcroft (London: G. G. J. and J. Robinson, 1779), 1:183.

15. The Greek phrase *kalos kagathos* means "what is inextricably beautiful and good."

16. Lavater, *Essays on Physiognomy,* 3:110.

17. Ibid., 3:197.

18. Ibid., 3:85.

19. G. W. Hegel, *Phenomenology of Spirit,* trans. A. V. Miller (Oxford: Oxford University Press, 1977), 191–93.

20. G. Ch. Lichtenberg, *Aphorismes,* trans. M. Robert (Paris: Club français du livre, 1947), 106.

21. Ibid., 162.

22. See Jacques Proust, "Diderot et la physionomie," *Cahiers de l'association internationale des études françaises,* June 1961, 317–29.

23. Hegel, *Phenomenology of Spirit,* 194.

24. Lavater, *Physiognomy,* 1:166.

25. Ibid., 3:2:391.

26. Ibid., 3:2:396.

27. Ibid., 3:2:393.

28. Ibid., 3:2:393–94.

29. Ibid., 3:2:396.

30. Jules Michelet, *Histoire de la Révolution française,* vol. 2, 1847–1853 (Paris: Gallimard Pléiade, 1979), 454–55.

31. François René de Chateaubriand, *Memoirs* (London: Henry Colburn, 1849), 410.

32. Roland Barthes, *Michelet,* trans. Richard Howard (Berkeley: University of California Press, 1992), 107, 113.

33. Michelet, *Histoire de la Révolution française,* 455. See also Jules Michelet, *L'oiseau* (Paris, 1856), pp. VIII, XLIII–XLIV.

34. Jules Michelet, *L'oiseau,* pp. VII and XLIV, and *Journal,* ed. P. Vialleneix (Paris: Gallimard, 1959), 1:621.

35. Tzvetan Todorov, *On Human Diversity,* trans. Catherine Porter (Cambridge, Mass.: Harvard University Press, 1998); Irène Tieder, "Michelet, la tradition révolutionnaire et les juifs," *Les nouveaux cahiers,* no. 120 (Spring 1995): 57–61.

36. Charles Dickens published the book of this title in 1854. [The song "Le temps des cerises" dates from 1868. This song, with words by Jean-Baptiste Clément and music by Antoine Renard, has become associated with the 1871 Paris Commune—Trans.]

37. See Xavier Tilliette, *Schelling, une philosophie en devenir* (Paris: Vrin, 1971), 1:446 n3, 411–14. We owe the neologism to both K. Ph. Moritz and Goethe.

38. Alphonse Toussenel, *L'esprit des bêtes,* vol. 1, *Ornithologie passionnelle,* 3.

39. Toussenel, *Zoologie passionnelle,* 372.

40. This is Simone Weil's word, though she uses it in an entirely different sense.

41. Toussenel, *Ornithologie passionnelle,* 1:188.

42. Dolf Oehler, *Le Spleen contre l'oubli, juin 1848 (Baudelaire, Flaubert, Heine, Herzen)* (Paris: Payot, 1996), 195–216.

43. Walter Benjamin, *The Arcades Project,* trans. Howard Eiland and Kevin McLaughlin (Cambridge, Mass.: Harvard University Press, 1999), 192 *sq.*

44. Toussenel, *Zoologie passionnelle,* 287.

45. Toussenel, *Ornithologie passionnelle,* 3:171.

46. Cited in the preface to the 1866 edition of *Les juifs rois de l'époque: Histoire de la féodalité financière* (Paris), iii.

47. Ibid., xxv. A book published under the same title in 1846 was much more nuanced than Toussenel's book. Its author was a Christian socialist, Pierre Leroux, who nonetheless reiterated the Académie's definition.

48. Cited in Leon Poliakov, *The History of Anti-Semitism,* vol. 3, *From Voltaire to Wagner,* trans. Miriam Kochan (Philadelphia: University of Pennsylvania Press, 2003).

49. Charles Fourier, *Theory of the Four Movements,* ed. and trans. Gareth Stedman Jones and Ian Patterson (Cambridge: Cambridge University Press, 1996), 191–281. See also *La Fausse Industrie morcelée, répugnante, mensongère et son antidote: L'industrie naturelle, combinée, attrayante, véridique, donnant quadruple produit* (Paris, 1836), 484–86.

50. Toussenel, *Les juifs rois de l'époque,* 124.

51. Toussenel, *Passional Zoology,* 167. [This nineteenth-century translation offers the term "usurer" as a translation for Toussenel's "juif." I have modified the translation to make Fontenay's point clear.—Trans.]

52. Ibid., 230–31, translation modified.

53. "Chaylok, Chaylok, I know you by my hatred," in Toussenel, *Ornithologie passionnelle,* 250–55. [My translation—Trans.]

54. Ibid, 3:234.

55. Ibid., 63.

56. Porphyry, *On Abstinence from Killing Animals,* trans. Gillian Clark (Ithaca: Cornell University Press, 2000), 1:16; Carl von Linné, *L'Equilibre de la nature* (1744–60, repr., Paris: Vrin, 1972).

57. Engels, *Dialectics of Nature.*

58. André Siegfried, *Tableau politique de la France de l'Ouest,* vol. 1 (Paris: Armand Colin, 1913).

5. They are Sleeping and We Are Watching over Them

1. A vicious circle of reciprocal inference.

2. Horkheimer and Adorno, *The Dialectic of Enlightenment,* 245.

3. Ibid., 246.

4. Ibid., 246–47.

5. Ibid.

6. Ibid.

7. Jacques Brunschwicg, "L'homme et l'animal dans la biologie d'Aristote," in fascicule V of Leon Poliakov's seminar, EHESS.

8. Labarrière, "De la phronèsis animale," 405–28.

9. See Porphyry, *On Abstinence from Killing Animals,* 3:10, 433, b29.

10. Ibid., 3:10, 433a.

11. I am borrowing this analysis from Labarrière, "De la phronèsis animale."

12. Aristotle, *On the Soul,* 3:10, 433 ab.

13. A monad is a simple substance, in other words, one without parts, that combines to form composites.

14. G. W. Leibniz, *New Essays on Human Understanding,* trans. and ed. Peter Remnant and Jonathan Bennett (New York: Cambridge University Press, 1996), 2:1: §§ 10, 11, 12.

15. G. W. Leibniz, *Die Philosophischen Schriften* (Berlin: Ed. Gerhardt, 1875–1890), 4:423, and *New Essays* 2:9: § 11.

16. Leibniz, *Die Philosophischen Schriften* 4:565.

17. Leibniz, *New Essays* 2:9: §12.

18. Ibid., 2:9: §14.

19. Ibid., 4:16: §12.

20. G. W. Leibniz, *Theodicy,* trans. E. M. Huggard (Charleston: Bibliobazaar, 2007), §91.

21. Ibid.

22. Ibid., §397.

23. I must recognize my debt to Françoise Dastur here, whose article in *Alter* entitled "Comment ne pas parler de l'animal" (How not to speak about the animal) was very enlightening. I must also acknowledge the editors of the journal *Alter* who translated and commented on Husserl's texts on animality. And finally, two other authors, whose dissertations were a great help to me in this project: Anne Montavont, *De la passivité dans la phénoménologie de Husserl* (Paris: PUF, 1999); and Bruce Bégout, *La généalogie de la logique* (Paris: Vrin, 2000).

24. Françoise Dastur, *Husserl, des mathématiques à l'histoire* (Paris: PUF, 1999).

25. Edmund Husserl, cited in *Alter,* "L'animalité," 1995, 194.

26. Ibid., 201.

27. Ibid.

28. Ibid., 202.

29. Ibid., 203 (emphasis mine).

30. Ibid.

6. The Pathetic Pranks of Bio-Art

1. Cited by Jens Hauser, "Gènes, genie, genes," in Jens Hauser, *L'art biotech* (Nantes: Le lieu unique, 2003), 9–15.

2. Ibid.

3. Eduardo Kac, cited in *Québec Sciences,* September 1999.

4. Genesis 1:28.

5. [The French Institut Scientifique de Recherche Agronomique, or Scientific Institute for Agronomic Research—Trans.]

6. Olivier Cadiot, *Retour définitif et durable de l'être aimé* (Paris: POL, 2002), 16.

7. See Philippe Dagen, *L'art impossible* (Paris: Grasset, 2002), 207–8.

8. Interview with Eduardo Kac, *Le Monde interactif,* December 15, 2000.

9. [See http://www.ekac.org/gfpbunny.html#gfpbunnyanchor—Trans.]

10. For the dog, see the story of Bobby in "The Name of a Dog, or Natural Rights," in Emmanuel Levinas, *Difficult Freedom: Essays on Judaism,* trans. Seàn Hand (Baltimore: Johns Hopkins University Press, 1997), 151–53. On the camel, see Emmanuel Levinas, *In the Name of the Nations,* trans. Michael B. Smith (London: Continuum, 2007), 120.

11. Martin Buber, *I and Thou,* trans. Walter Kaufman (Hesperides Press, 2008), 144–45: "The eyes of an animal have the capacity of a great language. . . . Undeniably, this cat began its glance by asking me with a glance that was ignited by the breath of my glance: 'Can it be that you mean me? . . . Am I there?'"

12. Merleau-Ponty, *Nature,* 197. [Translation slightly modified—Trans.]

13. Hans Jonas, *Evolution et Liberté,* (Paris: Payot et Rivages, 1999); and *The Phenomenon of Life: Toward a Philosophical Biology,* (Evanston, Ill.: Northwestern University Press, 2001).

14. Maurice Merleau-Ponty, *Résumés de cours au Collège de France* (Paris: Gallimard, 1968), 135–36.

15. Henri F. Ellenberger, "Jardin zoologique et hôpital psychiatrique," in *Médecines de l'âme: Essais d'historie de la folie et des guérisons psychiques* (Paris: Fayard, 1995). [Translated as "The Mental Hospital and the Zoological Garden," in *Animals and Man in Historical Perspective,* ed. Joseph Klaits and Barrie Klaits, 59–92 (New York: Harper and Row, 1974)—Trans.]

16. In a 1959 article by W. M. S. Russell and R. L. Burch [in *The Principles of Humane Experimental Technique* (London: Methuen, 1959)—Trans.], then V. Monamy (1996) ["Animal Experimentation: A Student Guide to Balancing the Issues," Australian and New Zealand Council for the Care of Animals in Research and Teaching—Trans.] and finally I. Vessier (1999, INRA) ["Expérimentation animale: biologie, éthique, réglementation," *INRA Productions Animales* 12 (December): 365–75; available at http://granit.jouy.inra.fr/productions-animales/1999/Prod_Anim_1999_12_5_03.pdf—Trans.].

7. The Ordinariness of Barbarity

1. Cf. Elisabeth Roudinesco, *Our Dark Side,* trans. David Macey (Cambridge: Polity, 2009).

2. In *Le silence des bêtes.*

3. Helvetius, *A Treatise on Man,* trans. W. Hooper, MD (London: Albion Press, 1810), 2:63.

4. Catherine and Raphaël Larrère, "Actualité de l'animal machine," *Les temps modernes,*no. 630–31 (March–June 2005): 145, 160–62.

5. Ibid., 149, 156.

6. Ibid. See also Florence Burgat, *L'animal dans les pratiques de consummation* (Paris: PUF, 1997).

7. See Georges Chapouthier, *Au bon vouloir de l'homme, l'animal* (Paris: Denoël, 1990).

8. Derrida, *The Animal That Therefore I Am,* 29.

Index

Born in 1934, **ÉLISABETH DE FONTENAY** was closely associated with the late Jacques Derrida and is professor emeritus of philosophy at the Sorbonne. She is the author of *Le silence des bêtes: La philosophie à l'épreuve de l'animalité* and *Diderot: Reason and Resonance.*

WILL BISHOP received his doctorate in French literature from the University of California, Berkeley. He lives in Paris, where he teaches and translates.